Arm
Knitting

Arm Knitting

30 no-needle projects for you and your home

DK

Contents

Introduction

Arm knitting – it's exactly what it sounds like. Instead of working with knitting needles, you knit on your arms. If you don't know how to knit, this is the perfect way to get acquainted with the craft. That's because it's easier than learning to manage cumbersome needles, but you still create the same stitches. If you're new to arm knitting, be warned: it's incredibly addictive – and fun for everyone.

Four reasons to arm knit

It's fast

Traditional knitting involves multiple stitches and different sizes of needles, but in arm knitting, your arms are like giant needles, and you typically use multiple strands of really thick yarn held together. Pairing big 'needles' and big yarns means you can create a lot of knitting with just one row. You'll be amazed at how quickly you can knit scarves, home décor, and many other objects.

It's easy

You don't need to have any previous knitting experience to arm knit. In fact, you can get away with learning just a single stitch: knit stitch. You can make many of the projects in this book with just that technique. If you become addicted – and you will – then you can try other stitches, such as purling, cabling, and yarnover.

It's fun

Arm knitting is enjoyable because you can almost effortlessly make a project in less than an hour, but it's also fun because you can experiment with many different fibres and stitches. You'll love choosing yarns and then seeing how they work up when you use a different number of strands. Success with arm knitting might even inspire you to design your own projects!

It's beautiful

Arm knitting is a great way to show off stunning chunky yarns. Because the stitches are large, they perfectly set off interesting textures. Your arm knitted accessories will look like they've been plucked right off the catwalk, while your arm knitted home décor will look cosy and stylish.

Arm knitting is something you'll definitely want to share with friends, discussing ideas and techniques, as well as knitting together. And because you can do this almost anywhere, it's perfect for socializing.

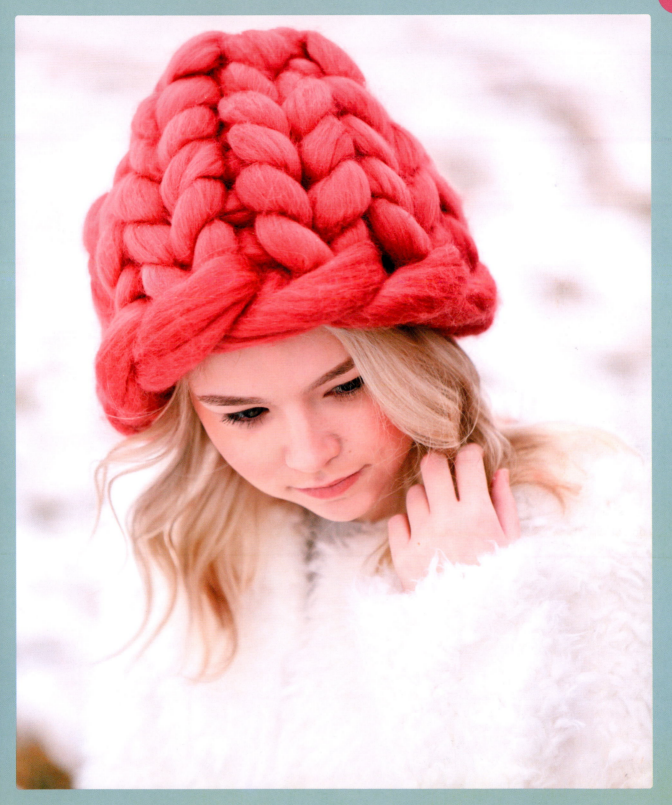

Materials, tools, and techniques

Arm knitting doesn't require much more than yarns in your favourite colours and, of course, your arms. The basic techniques described in this section will get you started on this new journey.

Yarns

Learning about the yarns that will work best for arm knitting will make this activity enjoyable. You'll have a chance to work with yarns of varying weights, including heavier yarns that are hard to use with needles, but are ideal for arms.

Fibres

The fibre you choose for a project depends on a couple of different factors. If you're arm knitting an item that needs frequent laundering, choose a superwash wool, or a washable cotton or acrylic. If you're on a budget, choose a low-cost synthetic yarn, so you can get more bulk at a lower price.

Animal fibre

Animal fibre can include anything from wool to alpaca to mohair. Animal fibre is perfect for winter accessories and garments. While such fibres are warm and luxurious, remember to diligently follow the care instructions.

You should wash most animal fibres in cold water and by hand. Otherwise, the fibres will felt together and ruin your beautiful stitches. If you want an animal fibre that's easier to care for, look for the word *superwash* on the label.

Plant fibre

Plant fibres include cotton, linen, and bamboo yarns. Because these fibres are strong and ideal for warmer temperatures, consider using them for such projects as home décor and summer accessories. Plant fibres also make good yarn substitutions for arm knitters who have an allergy to animal fibres.

Synthetic fibres and blends

Synthetic fibres, such as acrylic and nylon, are generally the easiest to care for. Synthetic yarn is a good choice if you're looking for a specific property. For example, if you want your project to have some elasticity, then a synthetic yarn with nylon in it is a good choice.

Synthetic yarns are also more budget-friendly. Novelty yarns, such as ribbon yarn, are slippery and can be difficult to work with, so gain some experience before arm knitting projects that use these fibres.

Unusual yarns

Several projects in this book give you a chance to arm knit with other kinds of yarns. Experiment with these materials, especially with projects that don't take long to make.

T-shirt yarn

T-shirt yarn is a stretchy material that's made from cotton, or a cotton blend. You can purchase T-shirt yarn online or from specialist knitting shops, or you can make your own T-shirt yarn at home by using jersey knit fabric from a haberdashery store, or using a T-shirt (or several) you no longer want. Do-it-yourself T-shirt yarn is a great choice for budget-conscious arm knitters.

Rope

Rope may seem like an unlikely candidate for arm knitting. However, thanks to its thickness and durability, it's a great choice for projects, particularly home décor. You can use any type of rope you'd like, but the most common rope fibres are cotton and synthetics, such as nylon.

Wool roving

Wool roving is a bulky fibre that's fuzzy and lofty. Because roving isn't plied, it doesn't have a twist to join the fibres like most yarns. You can buy it in knitting or craft shops, and online, packaged like other types of yarn, or in bags. You can also purchase roving in its natural state (often used for felting). You can separate roving by gently pulling the fibres apart to create a tapered edge that's easier to weave in. If the roving is difficult to pull apart, try holding your hands farther apart when you pull.

Packaging

Yarn is packaged in different types of bundles. If you purchase your yarn as a ball, skein, hank, or donut, no prep work is necessary before knitting. Some projects in this book will give you specific instructions about how to prepare your yarn for arm knitting.

Tools

Arm knitting doesn't require much more than your arms. Every pattern for the projects in this book lists any special tools needed. Collect all the tools and materials listed for a project before starting to knit, so you don't have to interrupt your work and figure out what to do with the stitches on your arms.

Essentials

Because this is arm knitting, you don't need knitting needles. But you'll always need scissors to trim yarn, and a ruler or tape measure.

Rulers

For all projects, you'll need to do some measuring. A quilting ruler lets you trim fringing to uniform lengths, while you'll find a short ruler and tape measure useful for measuring the length of work in progress and for checking tension.

Quilting ruler

Short ruler

Fabric scissors

Keep a Tool Kit Handy

Store all your arm knitting tools together in a bag or case so they're readily available when you begin an arm knitting project. If you have experience with conventional knitting and already own tools you like to use for any specific technique, feel free to use them for arm knitting if they're useful. And pop them in your arm knitting kit for future use.

Scissors

Any size scissors will do for cutting yarn. Only use your scissors to cut yarn and fabric, and have them sharpened regularly. Scissors used on paper become dull and will cut yarn or fabric in a ragged fashion.

Useful extras

Some projects, like those made from wool roving or those with seams, may require additional tools, but they're not necessary for all the patterns.

Stitch markers

If you're familiar with stitch markers for conventional knitting, note that you won't use them in the same way for arm knitting. Locking stitch markers can hold two pieces of knitted fabric that you need to seam together. You can also lock a marker around strands as a reminder to weave in the ends in that spot. Pipe cleaners or scrap yarn wrapped around strands can serve the same purpose.

Coloured stitch markers

Stitch holders

Stitch holders come in a variety of lengths. Use one to secure your work if you stop in the middle of a project; just open the holder, slip the stitches off your arm and onto it, and close it. If you don't have any, just slide your arm knitting onto a broom handle, piece of dowel, or a buckled belt.

Stitch holders in different sizes

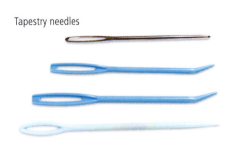

Pinking shears

Tapestry needles

These heavy, blunt needles each have a large eye for threading thick yarns. They're useful for seaming pieces of arm knitting together. You can also use them to weave in loose ends. They're optional – you can use your fingers to seam or weave instead – but it can make some tasks easier.

Tapestry needles

Pinking shears

These scissors produce a zigzag cut on fabric, which prevents unravelling. In this book, you'll only need them for projects that have a fabric lining.

Felting needles

These very sharp needles have barbed surfaces that compress wool fibres together to join them. You'll use these needles to secure cast-on and cast-off tails of wool roving to knitted work, or to join balls of wool roving.

Felting needles

Yarn weight chart

Yarn labels usually give information about thickness and weight. Many include a yarn symbol with a number on it. You should match your yarn weight to the specific weight listed for your project.

0	**Lace** 2-ply, Fingering
1	**Superfine** 3-ply, Fingering, Sock, Baby
2	**Fine** 4-ply, Sport, Baby
3	**Light** Double Knit (DK), Light Worsted
4	**Medium** Worsted, Afghan, Aran
5	**Chunky** Bulky, Craft, Rug
6	**Super chunky** Super Bulky, Wool Roving
7	**Wool roving** Jumbo, Giant

Yarn tension and weight

Yarn tension is the number of stitches and rows of knitting to a given measurement, often over a 10cm (4in) square. Your knitting must match the tension listed for each project to ensure you make the right size. This is easy with a ruler.

Understanding tension

Tension depends on three things: the diameter of the knitter's arms, the thickness of your yarn, and the number of strands held together. To control the finished size, you need to understand how to make adjustments. You don't generally need to worry too much about tension for something like a scarf or a necklace. However, it's critical for garments, where size is important to get the right fit.

The thickness of each yarn strand, as well as how many strands you hold together will also play a role in determining the tension. The thicker the yarn and the more strands of yarn you use, the fuller the arm knitting will be. For example, a project that uses 4 strands of super chunky yarn needs 8 strands of chunky yarn to achieve the same tension.

Check your tension

The diameter of every knitter's arms is different, so every knitter's stitches will be different. Each pattern states the number of stitches and rows per 10cm (4in) square. If your tension is larger than this, your finished project will be larger than the measurements given. If your tension is smaller, your finished project will be smaller than the measurements given. You may have to make adjustments to get the right size.

Wool roving   **Giant**   **Super chunky**   **Chunky**   **Aran**

Creating and using a tension swatch

Always create a tension swatch before knitting up your project to measure your tension with the yarn you selected and determine how to make modifications.

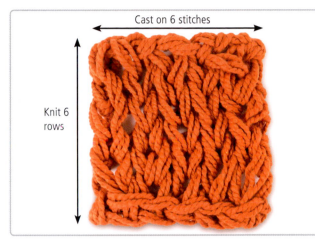

Cast on 6 stitches

Knit 6 rows

1 Cast on 6 stitches. Arm knit about 6 rows in the stitch the pattern uses. For example, if your project uses knit stitch, then knit each row. Cast off all the stitches.

In this tension swatch, 2.75 stitches equals 10cm (4in)

Measure near the centre

2 Place a ruler across the width of the swatch and then count the number of stitches for 10cm (4in). It's best to measure near the centre of the swatch to find the most accurate measurement.

In this tension swatch, 2.5 rows equals 10cm (4in)

3 Along the length of the swatch, count the number of rows in 10cm (4in). Compare your tension to the one listed in the project you want to make. Too many stitches and rows? Knit a new swatch with one less strand of yarn and measure the tension again. Too few stitches? Add a strand. Adjust until your tension matches.

Adjusting stitch size

You can't change the size of your arms, but one trick can adjust your tension: knitting stitches that are either looser or tighter. If you have too few rows or stitches, tighten the stitches on your arms as you knit. The smaller stitches this creates result in a smaller tension. If you have too many rows or stitches, do the opposite: loosen the stitches as you knit, giving the loops a little more wiggle room on your arm and making each stitch bigger.

Substituting yarn

You might sometimes need or want to use a different yarn to the one a project calls for. Knowing how to substitute yarn will help you select the appropriate replacement fibre.

Same weight, different yarn

Every project in this book lists the specific materials used, so you can replicate it exactly. You'll find this information at the very bottom of the 'Essential information' column. Each project also offers generic information so you can substitute the yarns you want. It's simplest to substitute a yarn in the same weight category as the designer's yarn. For example, if a project uses a super chunky yarn and you also use a super chunky yarn, you likely won't have to adjust your tension.

Different yarn weights

If you want to use a yarn in a different weight category, all you need to do is alter the number of strands. For example, if the project uses 4 strands of super chunky yarn, it might require 10 strands of a lighter chunky yarn. For this kind of substitution, you'll definitely need to make a swatch to check your tension. The more strands you add to your project, the thicker the stitches will be and the bigger your tension; if you use fewer strands, then the project will feel and look lighter and have a smaller tension.

12 strands of chunky yarn

8 strands of chunky yarn

5 strands of super chunky yarn

10 strands of
chunky yarn

6 strands
of super
chunky yarn

4 strands
of super
chunky yarn

Adding loft to yarn

Some fibres, such as alpaca and mohair, have beautiful airy thicknesses that are perfect for soft, dreamy projects. Give a yarn that's not fuzzy some texture by gently untwisting several of the strands. This gives the fibre a thicker loft without substituting the yarn.

When **substituting yarn**, always knit up a **tension swatch** before you begin working on the actual project to make sure the tension of **the new yarn matches** the tension of the pattern.

These swatches have the same number of stitches and rows but different weights and strands. They're the same finished size and so have the same tension.

Starting techniques

Every arm knitting project begins with a slip knot and cast-on stitches. But before you start any project, gather all the materials and tools for it, and read the instructions completely through to familiarize yourself with all its techniques.

Making a slip knot

Creating a slip knot is how you'll start any arm knitting project. A slip knot secures the knitting to your arm, and it's also your first cast-on stitch.

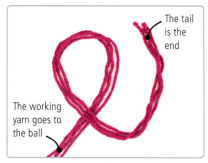

The tail is the end

The working yarn goes to the ball

1 Leaving a long tail for casting on (about 1.2m [47in] for every 10 stitches), cross the tail over the working yarn to create a circle.

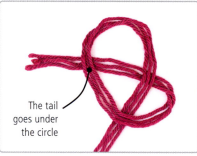

The tail goes under the circle

2 Place the tail under the circle, extending it across the centre.

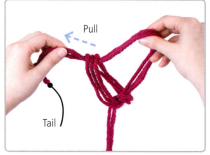

Pull

Tail

3 Hold the yarn tail with one hand and pull it tight, creating a loop at the centre of the circle.

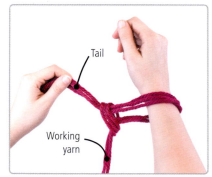

Tail

Working yarn

4 Place the loop on your right wrist, with the yarn tail in front facing you and the working yarn extending from the back.

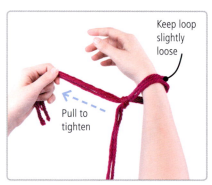

Keep loop slightly loose

Pull to tighten

5 Tighten the slip knot, but leave the loop on your wrist slightly loose. This counts as your first cast-on stitch.

Using Multiple Strands

When knitting with several strands of yarn together, it's easier to hold them as a single strand. To make this easier, tie a small knot in the tails of the working yarn to hold the ends together, then draw out the strands ready for use. When knitting, be sure to pick up all of the strands for each stitch.

Long-tail cast on

Once you've placed the slip knot, which serves as your first stitch, on your arm, you'll need to cast on additional stitches. Make sure the cast-on tail extends from the side of the wrist closest to you and the working yarn extends from the back.

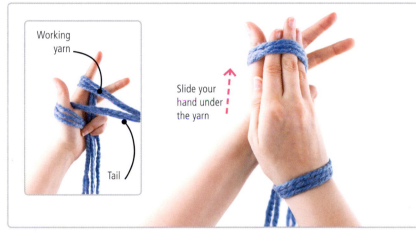

Working yarn

Slide your hand under the yarn

Tail

Working yarn

1 Place the yarn tail behind your left thumb, and place the working yarn behind your left index finger. Spread your fingers apart to create a 'sling shot' of yarn. Slide your right hand under the sling shot, entering from the side of your left thumb.

2 With your right hand, grab the working yarn that's wrapped around the front of your index finger.

Pull the loop onto your hand

Pull

6 5 4 3 2 1

3 Pull the loop through and onto your right hand.

4 Pull the working yarn and tail to tighten the loop, being careful to leave enough room to pull the loop off your hand when you begin knitting.

5 Repeat these steps to cast on the number of stitches required by the pattern, keeping in mind that your slip knot counts as the first cast-on stitch.

Stitches

The two foundation stitches of knitting are the knit stitch and the purl stitch. These two basic stitches can be combined to create different stitch patterns and textures. For some projects, you'll only knit. For others, you might only purl, or mix them up in various ways.

Knit stitch

Arm knitting's most basic stitch is knit stitch. With this stitch, you can create practically any project in this book.

Working yarn

Tail

1 Cast on the number of stitches you need.

Working yarn

2 Place the working yarn over your right thumb from front to back, with the tail moving away from you, and close your fingers over the yarn.

Working yarn

Cast-on stitch

3 Slip the cast-on stitch closest to the thumb off your arm and over your hand.

Cast-on stitch

Working yarn

4 Drop the cast-on stitch while still grasping the working yarn.

Working yarn

5 Slide your left hand under the loop on your right hand.

6 Slide this loop onto your left wrist. This twists the loop so the working yarn is in front.

Pull to tighten

7 Pull gently on the working yarn to tighten the stitch around your left arm.

The right side faces you

8 Repeat steps 2 to 7 until you've moved all the stitches from one arm to the other.

Carry on...

To knit the next row, repeat these steps, but this time, move the stitches from your left arm back to your right arm. The rows of knitting will continue like this, moving back and forth from arm to arm. The right side of the work will always face you.

Front leg vs. back leg

The side of the stitch that faces you is called the *front leg* of the stitch. When the knitted stitches are on your left arm, the right side of the loop will be the front leg. When the stitches are on your right arm, the left side of the loop should always be the front leg. If you reverse this, your knit stitches will create a twist at the base.

Front

Back

Stocking stitch

When you're arm knitting, the right side of the work always faces you. If you knit every row, you'll knit what's called *stocking* *stitch*. This creates a piece with V stitches on the right side and bumps on the wrong side.

Each V is a stitch – count them up the centre to count rows

Bumps identify the wrong side

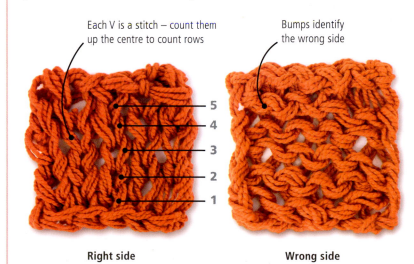

5
4
3
2
1

Right side

Wrong side

Purl stitch

Purl stitch is the sister stitch to knit stitch. Adding it to your repertoire opens up the opportunity for special stitches with interesting textures, such as moss stitch and rib stitch. You should become as familiar with this stitch as with knit stitch.

Working yarn

Stitch 2

Stitch 1

1 Place the working yarn from front to back across your arm in the space between the first two stitches closest to your hand, and then let go of the working yarn.

Pull the working yarn through

Stitch 1

Stitch 2

2 Reach through the first stitch, grabbing the working yarn with your left hand and pulling the working yarn through to create a new stitch.

New stitch

Working yarn

Pull your right hand out to drop the old stitch

3 Drop the old stitch off your right arm.

4 Place the new stitch on to your opposite arm.

5 Pull on the working yarn to tighten the loop.

6 Repeat steps 1 to 5 until you've moved all the stitches from one arm to the other.

Carry on...

To purl the next row, repeat these steps, but this time, move the stitches from your left arm to your right arm. Continue the rows of purling in this manner, moving back and forth from arm to arm, with the right side of the work always facing you.

tip

Always make sure the working yarn is extending from the front leg of the stitch. Otherwise, your stitches will twist.

Garter stitch

Once you learn purl stitch, you can create garter stitch. Garter stitch alternates knit and purl rows, creating a knitted piece with a different texture from the stocking stitch pattern you create by knitting all the rows.

Finishing

When you've finished arm knitting, you'll need to close the stitches and remove them from your arms so they don't unravel. After that, you'll also need to secure the ends by either weaving them in, or needle felting them.

Casting off

Cast off closes the stitches so they don't come apart. It's similar to knitting, except you'll remove the stitches from your arm as you work across the row.

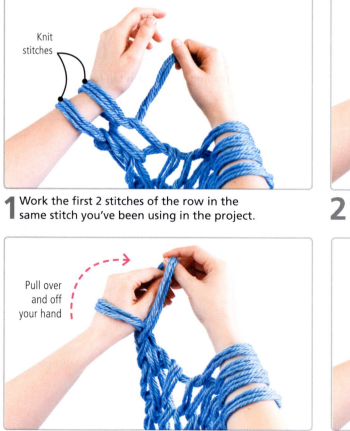

Knit stitches

1 Work the first 2 stitches of the row in the same stitch you've been using in the project.

2 Grasp the stitch closest to your left elbow.

Pull over and off your hand

3 Pull that stitch over the stitch closest to your left hand, and then pull it off your left arm.

4 Drop the stitch. You should now have only 1 stitch remaining on your left arm.

Working yarn

Knit stitch

5 Work another stitch on your right arm. You'll have 2 stitches on your left arm.

6 Grasp the stitch closest to your left elbow and pull it over the stitch closest to your left hand, then pull it off your left arm. Keep repeating steps 5 and 6 until only 1 stitch remains on your left arm. Cut the working yarn, leaving a long yarn tail for weaving in.

Last stitch

A cast-off end looks like a plait at the edge of the knitting

Yarn tail

7 Remove the stitch from your left wrist and then pull the yarn tail through the loop of the last stitch. Pull the yarn tight to secure it.

tip

Make sure the cast-off row matches the project's stitches. For example, if you work the project in moss stitch, then your cast-off row also needs to be in moss stitch.

Weaving in ends

You'll need to weave any tails from casting on, casting off, or adding new yarns into the project to hide and secure them. If you have a project with seams, use your cast-on or cast-off tail to seam first, and then weave in the ends. If your project calls for multiple strands of yarn held together while knitting, weave them in together.

Tail

1 Working on the wrong side of the work, weave the tail (shown in orange) through the nearest stitch.

Weave the tail through the stitches

2 Following the shape of the adjacent stitches, weave the tail through the stitches.

tip

You can thread a tapestry needle with a long tail to weave it in, but it's easier to use your hand.

Tuck the tail into one of the nearest stitches

3 Keep weaving until you've woven in the entire tail, then tuck the end into one of the nearest stitches to secure it.

Variation

Weave the yarn tail in and out of the cast-off edge, cast-on edge, or, if your project has one, through the seam where the work is tightest and most durable.

Needle felting wool roving

Wool roving benefits from a special finishing method to ensure the yarn tails don't come loose. The technique of felting interlocks the roving fibres together. You can use it to join any yarn tails to the stitches near them, so they'll permanently stay in place.

What you'll need

- Thick foam pad or needle felting mat
- Felting needle

Yarn tail

1 Place the knitted piece right side down on a thick foam pad, or on a needle felting mat. Place the yarn tail (shown in blue) to be needle felted on top of adjacent stitches, allowing an overlap of about 8cm (3in).

Pierce 6mm (¼in) deep

2 Lightly pierce the felting needle straight up and down through both layers of wool roving, piercing about 6mm (¼in) deep into the stitches.

3 Continue to pierce the yarn tail with the needle until the tail is compressed firmly and securely into the stitches.

Seaming

Seaming is how you connect two pieces of arm knitting. There are two methods used in this book, whip stitch and mattress stitch. The project instructions will tell you which to use.

Whip stitch

This seaming technique creates a stitch that's sturdy and functional, but not stretchy. It's visible even when using the same colour yarn as the knitting because it wraps around the edges of two pieces. It looks decorative when you use a different colour.

Wrong sides together

1 Place two knitted pieces on top of each other, with the wrong sides together and the edge stitches lined up evenly. The seaming yarn will be the tail of the bottom piece.

Seaming yarn

2 Insert the seaming yarn (shown in orange) from the bottom to the top through the bottom-right corner stitch of both pieces. (If you're using separate yarn rather than an existing tail, leave a long tail for weaving in later.)

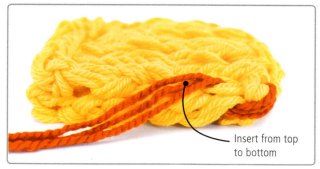

Insert from top to bottom

3 Insert the seaming yarn from the bottom to the top of the next set of stitches. The seaming yarn will wrap around the outside of the work.

Line up the top and bottom pieces evenly

4 Repeat step 3, working your way up the seam and lining up the stitches as evenly as possible, until you've seamed the entire edge.

Mattress stitch

This stretchy stitch creates a barely visible seam on the right side of the work when you use the same colour yarn used for the knitting. Take care to line up the pieces side by side.

Right sides up

1 Place the two knitted pieces side by side, with the right sides up (unless the project instructions say to arrange them differently).

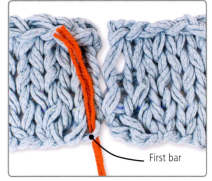

First bar

2 Stretch the side edges of both pieces to reveal the small 'bars' that run side to side. Insert the seaming tail (shown in orange) under the first bar on the left piece.

First bar

3 Insert the seaming tail under the first bar on the right piece.

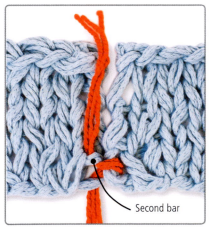

Second bar

4 Insert the seaming tail under the second bar on the left piece.

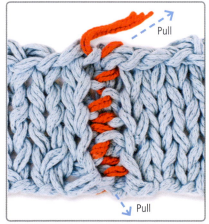

Pull

Pull

5 Continue weaving the seaming tail under the next bar, moving from side to side. When you finish seaming the entire edge, pull on each end of the seam to hide the seaming yarn, then weave in any loose ends.

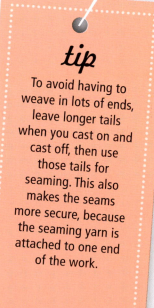

tip

To avoid having to weave in lots of ends, leave longer tails when you cast on and cast off, then use those tails for seaming. This also makes the seams more secure, because the seaming yarn is attached to one end of the work.

Adding more yarn

What do you do if you find that your ball has run out of yarn, or that you'd like to change the colour you're using to knit some rows in another shade? You can use the spit splice and joining in techniques.

Spit splice

If you're knitting with 100% animal fibres, like 100% wool or alpaca, you can literally join both of the yarn ends into a single strand using a spit splice. Note that this technique works best for joining together yarns in the same colour.

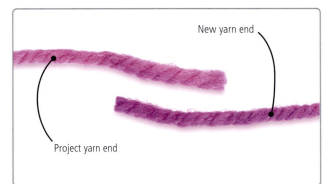

New yarn end

Project yarn end

1 To join new yarn of the same colour as your working yarn, start with the end from your project and one from the new yarn.

Untwist the yarn ends

2 Untwist about 8cm (3in) of the plies on each yarn end and then overlap them, with the tails going in opposite directions.

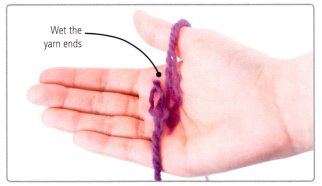

Wet the yarn ends

3 Soak the ends with water. Place the ends on one hand and then rub both palms together vigorously to agitate the ends.

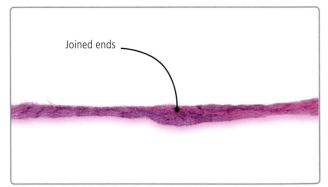

Joined ends

4 You can stop rubbing your hands together when the two ends look like a single strand of yarn, indicating that they've felted together.

Joining in yarns or changing colours

If you're working with a synthetic yarn, or a blend, and the ball runs out, or if you want to alternate colours to create stripes, you'll need to properly join the yarns so your stitches don't unravel. It's best to join yarns or change colours when you're ready to start a new row.

Grey yarn is being added to knitted pink yarn

Pull the first stitch over your right hand

tip

When you finish arm knitting your project, weave in the tails of the new and old yarns into the wrong side.

1 At the beginning of a new row, hold the new yarn with your left hand, leaving a tail about 25.5cm (10in) long, and then knot the new yarn loosely around the working yarn to secure it.

2 While holding the new yarn in your right hand, take the first stitch of the row and begin to pull it over your hand.

First stitch of the row

New stitch

3 Pull the first stitch of the row completely over your hand and let it drop off.

4 Place the new stitch on your left arm. Continue knitting as usual, using the new yarn.

Decreasing

Decreasing combines two stitches into one to shape the work. (Increases are also used for shaping, but not in this book.) The two decreasing methods result in stitches that lean in different directions – which direction depends on which arm the stitch is on.

Knit 2 together

This decrease is almost identical to a knit stitch, except you'll pick up and drop 2 stitches instead of 1.

Working yarn

1 Knit until you reach the place where you want to decrease. End with the working yarn over your right thumb, as if you were going to knit the next stitch.

Pull both stitches over at the same time

2 Pull 2 stitches over your hand (rather than 1 stitch, which is what you would do for a knit stitch).

New stitch

3 Put the new loop on your arm. You've decreased 1 stitch. Continue knitting as usual.

tip
As the project instructions will tell you which decreasing method to use, you need to become proficient in both.

Slip, slip, knit

Slip, slip, knit results in a decrease that leans in the opposite direction to a knit 2 together decrease.

Front leg of the stitch

1 Knit until you reach the place where you want to decrease and then slip the next 2 stitches, one at a time from one arm to the other, twisting the loops so the right side of the loop becomes the front leg.

Working yarn

2 Lay the working yarn from front to back over your left thumb.

Pull the two slipped stitches over

3 Pull the 2 slipped stitches over your hand and drop them. You have decreased 1 stitch.

Leaning stitches: Comparing knit 2 together with slip, slip, knit

Knit 2 together slants to the right when you're working from your left arm to your right, and to the left if you're working from your right arm to your left.

Slip, slip, knit slants to the left when you're working from your left arm to your right, and to the right when you're working from your right arm to your left.

When decreasing, the stitches on the left edge should lean right into the centre, while the stitches on the right edge should lean left into the centre.

Stitches slanting to the right

Knit 2 together worked from the left arm to the right.

Stitches slanting to the left

Slip, slip, knit worked from the left arm to the right.

Additional techniques

Despite being easy, arm knitting does have a couple of tricks you can use to further simplify some techniques. These two methods are used in only a handful of projects in this book, but for those few, they're indispensable.

Chain plying technique

This technique allows you to create 3 strands from one ball of yarn. You'll avoid having to knit with multiple balls, which can result in tangled strands.

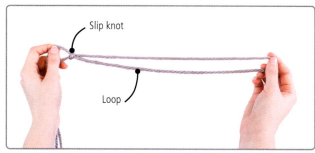

1 Make a slip knot, pulling the yarn loop until it's about 30cm (12in) long.

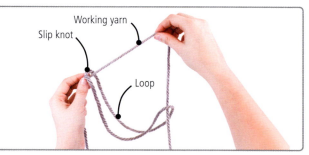

2 Holding the slip knot and tail in your left hand, reach through the loop with your right hand to pull up on the working yarn, drawing it through the loop to create a second loop, about 30cm (12in) long.

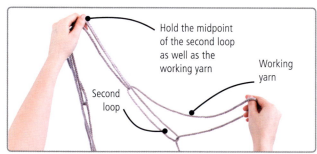

3 Drop the slip knot, and use your left hand to hold all 3 strands halfway along the length of the second loop. Reach through the right end of the loop to draw out the working yarn to create a third loop, 30cm (12in) long. Repeat this step to chain ply the entire ball.

Concealed loops

Knitting made with this plying technique looks the same as if you've held 3 strands together from 3 different balls of yarn. The loops created during the plying process aren't noticeable because they are camouflaged by the many strands and stitches in the knitting.

Picking up stitches

Picking up stitches allows you to create new loops on the edges of a knitted piece.
It's great for creating shape and definition, or when adding additional length.

1 Hold the knitted piece right side up, with the edge you want to pick up stitches from at the top.

2 Place your hand through the centre of the first V-shaped stitch and grasp your working yarn. Leaving a long tail for weaving in later, pull the working yarn through the stitch, creating a loop.

3 Place the loop on your right arm, with the working yarn extending from the stitch's front leg.

4 Place your right hand through the centre of the next V-shaped stitch and pull up another loop.

5 Place the loop on your right arm once again, with the working yarn extending from the stitch's front leg.

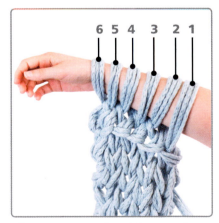

6 Repeat steps 4 and 5 across the edge, pulling up a loop from each V-shaped stitch until you've picked up the number of stitches instructed in the pattern.

Head to toe

From hats and scarves to bags and boot cuffs, these projects offer various accessories to complement your everyday look. You'll also learn to make a fringe and pompoms.

Twisted scarf

Rather than being knitted from plied yarn, this scarf uses a yarn knitted as a netted tube. This gives the fibre more loft and bulk, making it perfect for arm knitting.

Essential information

Difficulty level
Easy

Time to make
20 minutes

Finished size
1.2m (48in) long

Materials
24m (26 yds) of super chunky netted acrylic-blend yarn

Tools
Scissors

Tension
2 stitches and 2 rows equal 10cm (4in).

This project was made with 2 balls of Premier Yarns Couture Jazz in Pumpkin Pie, 15m (16.5 yds).

Wear this scarf by tucking one end through a knit stitch one third of the way up the scarf's length.

How to make

Magic knot

The purpose of this nearly invisible knot is to connect the 2 balls of yarn into one single piece of yarn before you start knitting. That way, you'll have fewer ends to weave in later.

1 Pull one end out from each ball and then place them on your work surface, with the tails facing in opposite directions.

2 Tie one tail around the other and tie the loose tail around the other working yarn, as shown in Figure 1, then loosely tighten the knots.

3 Holding the working yarns, pull gently in opposite directions until the knots slide together.

4 Pull the knots tight and then trim the tail ends close to the knot.

Scarf

1 Cast on 4 stitches.

2 Arm knit until you have approximately 1m (39in) of working yarn left.

3 Cast off all the stitches, leaving a 25.5cm (10in) yarn tail.

Making up

At each end of the scarf, tie the long tail into a loop on the inside of the scarf and then cut the remaining yarn, or weave it into the scarf.

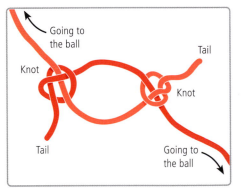

Figure 1 In the second step of making a magic knot, tie each tail around the other.

Keep the stitches **consistently tight** on your arms to ensure even stitches that **aren't too large**.

tip

You can create a striped effect with two colours by using multiple magic knots to attach several colours of yarn together.

tip

Try on the boot cuffs as you arm knit them, and before you add the buttons, to ensure a snug fit around your calf.

Boot cuffs

Choose plant-based or synthetic yarn to make these funky accessories. Animal fibres will felt together if they rub against your boots, causing the cuffs to bobble.

How to make

Cuffs (make 2)

1 Cast on 6 stitches.

2 Arm knit in stocking stitch until the cuff measures 46cm (18in) long when blocked, or the desired length plus 2.5cm (1in). Before you measure the length, stretch out the cuff lengthwise.

3 Cast off all the stitches, and weave in all the ends.

Making up

Sew 2 buttons to the short edge of the right side of each boot cuff. To hide the sewing thread, use your fingers to unroll the T-shirt yarn and then sew the button there. When you finish, the yarn will roll back up, hiding the trimmed sewing thread.

Choose buttons that either stand out against the yarn you use, or ones that match the cuffs, depending on the look you'd like.

You can use a **different yarn** or a different number of **strands**, but make sure the cuff isn't **too bulky**. A bulky cuff might cause an **uncomfortable fit** when your boot goes over it.

Essential information

Difficulty level
Easy

Time to make
30 minutes

Finished size
11.5cm x 1.8m
(4½ x 72in)

Materials
114m (125 yds) of super
chunky yarn, with 3
strands held together

Tools
Scissors

Tension
2 stitches and 3.75 rows
equals 10cm (4in).

*This project was made with
1 bump of BagSmith Big
Stitch Merino in Multi
Fawn, 114m (125 yds).*

Infinity scarf

A yarn that resembles dreadlocks gives this infinity scarf its unique appearance. Wrap it twice around your neck for a casual look or three times for a super snug cowl.

How to make

Scarf

1 Cast on 4 stitches.

2 Arm knit until the piece measures approximately 1.8m (71in).

3 Cast off all the stitches.

4 Seam the cast-on and cast-off edges together.

5 Weave in and trim all the ends.

Creating a scarf is a great introduction to arm knitting: it doesn't take long to make; it's inexpensive; and you'll quickly enjoy knitting with your arms.

This scarf looks like it includes three different yarns in several different colours, but the designer actually achieved it by using a single multicoloured yarn.

tip

Making this scarf
with a neutral-
coloured yarn
allows you
to wear it with
myriad shades
of clothing.

tip

Placing the piece flat on a table to seam it will result in a neater and less bulky seam because you can line up the stitches more easily.

Mega cowl

Essential information

Difficulty level
Easy

Time to make
20 minutes

Finished size
71 x 30.5cm (28 x 12in)

Materials
38m (42 yds) of super chunky yarn, with 2 strands held together

Tools
Scissors

Tension
2 stitches and 1 row equals 10cm (4in).

This project was made with 2 balls of Loops & Threads Biggie in Dark Grey, 19m (21 yds).

Keeping the stitches tight as you arm knit will give this cowl more durability.

Mega cowl

You'll arm knit this soft, cosy cowl in no time! Made with a luxurious roving-like yarn, this delightful accessory will keep the compliments coming – and the chill away.

How to make

Cowl

1 Cast on 6 stitches.

2 Arm knit until the piece measures 71cm (28in) long.

3 Cast off all the stitches, leaving a 46cm (18in) yarn tail.

4 Place the piece on your work surface, wrong side up, and then seam the edges by using whip stitch.

5 Weave in all the ends.

Whip stitch the seam carefully so it's barely visible, no matter how you wear this cowl.

Try leaving the cowl **unseamed**. Instead, sew a **large decorative button** on one of the edge corners. You don't need to make a buttonhole, simply **slide the button** through any **open stitch**.

Essential information

Difficulty level
Easy

Time to make
10 minutes

Finished size
43 x 12.5cm (17 x 5in)

Materials
291m (318 yds) of super chunky yarn, with 3 strands held together

Tools
Scissors

Tension
4 stitches and 2 rows equals 10cm (4in).

This project was made with 3 balls of Lion Brand Yarns Wool-Ease Thick & Quick in Blossom, 97m (106 yds).

Choose colours for this ear warmer that match your seasonal outfits.

Ear warmer

Need a last-minute gift? One that's not only fast and easy to arm knit but is also fun to wear? Made with a soft, cosy yarn, this pretty accessory meets all those desires.

How to make

Ear warmer

1 Cast on 6 stitches.

2 Arm knit until the piece measures approximately 43cm (17in) long.

3 Cast off all the stitches.

4 Seam the short ends together by using whip stitch.

5 Weave in all the ends.

Before you seam the short edges together, make sure the piece isn't twisted.

After you **finish arm knitting** to the stated length, **try this** on your head **before casting off** all the stitches.

tip

To make this ear warmer extra thick and cosy, hold together 4 or 5 strands of a super chunky yarn.

tip

You can make the fringe as long or as short as you like – just make incremental cuts until you feel it's the perfect length.

Essential information

Difficulty level
Moderate

Time to make
90 minutes

Finished size
20.5cm x 2.3m (8 x 91in)

Materials
349m (382 yds) of super chunky yarn, with 3 strands held together

Tools
Stitch holder
Scissors
Measuring tape

Tension
3 stitches and 2 rows equals 10cm (4in).

This project was made with 7 skeins of Plymouth Yarn Baby Alpaca Magna in 3317 Tiffany, 51m (55 yds).

Cable scarf

If you're keen to use a luxury yarn, this is the project for it. This scarf is easy to make, and it's versatile because you can drape it over your shoulders or wear it as a wrap.

How to make

Scarf

1 Cast on 8 stitches.

2 Stitch row: Purl the first 2 stitches, knit the next 4 stitches, and purl the last 2 stitches.

3 Cable row: Purl the first 2 stitches, and then slip the next 2 stitches onto the stitch holder, as shown in Figure 1.

Slip the stitches on the stitch holder off your arm and place them at the back of the piece. Arm knit the next 2 stitches. Place the stitches from the stitch holder back onto your arm, as shown in Figure 2, and then knit these 2 stitches.

Purl the last 2 stitches of the row.

4 Continue knitting, alternating between the stitch and cable rows, until the scarf measures 2.3m (91in), or your desired length.

5 Cast off the stitches, and weave in all the ends.

Figure 1 Place the next two stitches to be worked onto a stitch holder, then slide the stitches over your hand and off your arm.

Figure 2 Place the two stitches on the stitch holder back over your hand and onto your arm, then remove the stitch holder.

Continued ➡

Fringe

1 Cut forty-eight 51cm (20in) strands of yarn.

2 Form the fringe by holding 3 strands of yarn together and folding the strands in half, forming a loop at the top.

3 Slide the loop through the first stitch of the cast-on edge.

4 Slip the fringe tails through the loop.

5 Pull tight on the fringe tails to secure the fringe.

6 Repeat this fringe process across the cast-on and cast-off edges. Trim the fringe evenly.

*See the **Making a fringe** section for more specific instructions.*

Choose a light colour for this scarf to help spotlight and define the cable that runs down the centre.

This long scarf could easily be used as a cowl or an infinity scarf. Knit to the length you'd like and then seam the cast-on and cast-off edges together – and, of course, leave off the fringe.

tip

This scarf can feel heavy as you arm knit. Use a flat surface to hold it as you work. This will take some of the weight off your arms.

Making a fringe

A fringe is a great embellishment for scarves and rugs. Customize it as thick, long, and luxuriously as you like. You can also select a different colour to the one used for the main part of the project; attaching a fringe in alternate colours, or mixing several hues.

What you'll need

- Scissors
- Yarn specified by the project instructions
- Ruler

Cut all the strands first

1 Cut the strands of yarn as instructed by the pattern. (The instructions will tell you how many strands and how long each strand should be.)

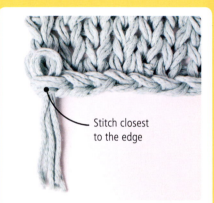

Stitch closest to the edge

3 Slide the loop under the first stitch closest to the edge.

6 Repeat steps 2 to 5 across the edges where you want a fringe.

2 Hold together the number of strands mentioned in the project instructions and then fold the strands in half, forming a loop on one side.

Fringe Modifications

To make your fringe look and feel thicker than the one shown for a project, just cut more strands of yarn in step 1, and then add additional strands to each stitch in steps 2 to 6. For a longer fringe, in step 1, cut the yarn twice as long as the desired finished length, plus 2.5cm (1in) extra.

Bring the tails up and then through the loop

4 Pull the fringe tails through the loop.

Pull the tails to tighten them

5 Pull the fringe tails tight to secure them.

Trim the ends

7 Use scissors to trim the fringe ends evenly.

tip

To keep the fringe ends even, place a ruler across the entire fringe to use as a guide as you cut.

Essential information

Difficulty level
Moderate

Time to make
90 minutes

Finished size
40.5 x 38cm (16 x 15in)

Materials
161m (176 yds) of super chunky yarn, with 6 strands held together (or 2 strands held together if using the chain plying technique)

Sewing thread

Tools
Scissors
Sewing needle

Tension
2 stitches and 3.75 rows equals 10cm (4in).

This project was made with 2 skeins of Premier Craft-Tee Yarn in Light Grey Shades, 81m (88 yds).

Bento bag

Based loosely on a Japanese design, this bag has an asymmetrical structure that looks symmetrical once assembled. It folds flat but actually holds a lot.

How to make

Bag

1 Cast on 8 stitches, leaving a 38cm (15in) yarn tail for seaming.

2 Arm knit 23 rows, or until the piece measures approximately 81.5cm (32in).

3 Cast off all the stitches. Cut the yarn, leaving a 38cm (15in) yarn tail.

You can line your bag by tacking fabric to the knit piece before seaming the bag together, and then sew the fabric permanently to the edges after assembling the bag.

This isn't your usual handbag, but that's what will make a statement, especially when you tell people you made it with your arms.

Continued ➜

tip

Use the chain plying technique to turn 1 strand of yarn into 3 strands, so you don't have to hold 6 strands simultaneously.

You can give your bag a **different** feel by making your own yarn from stretchy T-shirt fabric.

Making up

1 Place the piece horizontally, wrong side up, on your work surface. Fold the left edge across the piece, so a section 18cm (7in) wide overlaps the rest of the piece, as shown in Figure 1. Using mattress stitch, seam only the bottom edges together along the 18cm (7in) overlap.

2 Unfold corner A down as far as possible towards the bottom-lefthand corner, as shown in Figure 2. Now fold the right edge across the piece, so an 18cm (7in)-wide section overlaps the

rest of the piece, as shown in Figure 3. (It might look messy, but keep going!) Using mattress stitch, seam only the 18cm (7in) upper edges together.

3 Using sewing thread and a needle, sew corners A and B to each other to make the handle.

*See the **Making T-shirt yarn** and **Chain plying technique** sections for more specific instructions.*

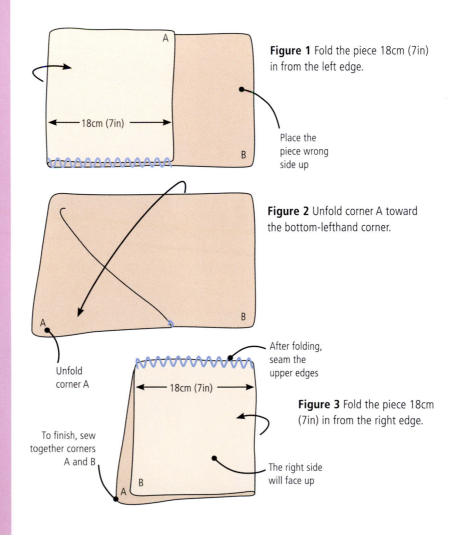

Figure 1 Fold the piece 18cm (7in) in from the left edge.

Place the piece wrong side up

Figure 2 Unfold corner A toward the bottom-lefthand corner.

Unfold corner A

After folding, seam the upper edges

Figure 3 Fold the piece 18cm (7in) in from the right edge.

To finish, sew together corners A and B

The right side will face up

18cm (7in)

Essential information

Difficulty level
Moderate

Time to make
45 minutes

Finished size
Chest: 71 (81:91:102) cm
(28 (32:36:40) in)

Materials
27cm to 55m (30 to 60 yds)
or 680g to 1.4kg (1.5 to 3lb)
of raw, unspun merino wool
roving with a 23-micron
count (or use giant chunky
yarn in the same weight)

Tools
Felting needle
Scissors

Tension
2 stitches and 3 rows equals
10cm (4in).

*This project was made with
1 ball of Intreccio Giant
Merino roving in Natural,
27m (30 yds).*

Boho gilet

This chunky cropped gilet is made as a single piece, except for two small seams at the shoulders. And it's also reversible, making it even more irresistible.

How to make

Gilet

Measure your bust. Referring to the finished size in the column, left, when following the instructions, use the number in the same position as your chest size.

1 Cast on 14 (16:18:20) stitches.

2 Arm knit 4 (5:6:7) rows of stocking stitch.

Front right side

1 Knit 1, knit 2 together. This is the beginning of the front right side, which now consists of 2 stitches. For now, work only with the 2 stitches you just knitted and leave the other 11 (13:15:17) stitches unworked.

2 Arm knit 7 (8:9:10) more rows of your 2-stitch front right side, and then cast off all the stitches on the right front.

3 Cut the wool roving/yarn to begin working on the centre back section of the garment, leaving a 38cm (15in) tail to stitch the front right side to the back section at the shoulders once you've completed the knitting.

Keep your stitches as tight as you can in order to create a solid texture for your gilet.

Because you have so few stitches to knit, you won't need to push them all the way up your arm.

Continued ➡

Centre back section

1 Return to the 11 (13:15:17) unworked stitches. Slip, slip, knit to decrease 1 stitch, knit 4 (6:8:10) stitches, knit 2 together. Leave the final 3 stitches unworked for the front left side. Continue working with the 6 (8:10:12) remaining stitches for the centre back section.

2 Arm knit 5 (6:7:8) rows of the centre back section, and then cast off. Cut the wool roving/yarn to begin working on the second front side. You don't need to leave a tail.

Front left side

1 Return to the 3 remaining stitches. Slip, slip, knit to decrease 1 stitch, knit 1. The front left side now has 2 stitches.

2 Arm knit 7 (8:9:10) more rows of the 2-stitch front left side, and then cast off. Cut the wool roving/yarn, leaving a 38cm (15in) tail to stitch the front and back pieces together at the shoulders later.

Join the shoulders

Use your fingers and the yarn tails to stitch the tops of the front sides to the 2 outside stitches on either side of the centre back section, as shown in Figure 1. You'll join A to A, B to B, C to C, and D to D.

Making up

Trim all the ends of the wool roving/yarn to about 20.5cm (8in) long, and then weave in or needle felt the ends of the wool roving/yarn into the gilet to ensure they permanently stay in place.

*See the **Needle felting wool roving** section for more specific instructions.*

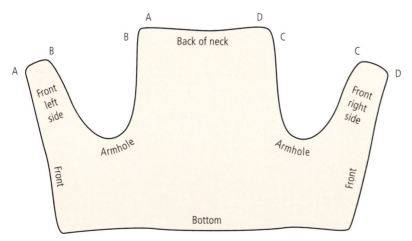

Figure 1 Join A and B on the front left side to A and B on the back of the neck and then join C and D on the front right side to C and D on the back of the neck.

tip

You'll use the tails left after making the front pieces to join the shoulders. You don't need a needle – just use your fingers.

Essential information

Difficulty level
Moderate

Time to make
20 minutes

Finished size
51cm (20in) circumference

Materials
14m (15 yds) or 340g (12oz) of raw, unspun merino wool roving with a 23-micron count (or use giant yarn in the same weight)

Tools
Felting needle
Scissors

Tension
2 stitches and 3 rows equals 10cm (4in).

This project was made with 1 ball of Intreccio Giant Merino roving in Dusty Rose, 18m (20 yds).

Quirky hat

This hat is the perfect beginner project because it knits up fast and lets you practise a new skill: decreasing. Making this hat in wool roving results in a structured shape.

How to make

Hat

1 Cast on 12 stitches.

2 Arm knit 1 row.

Row 2: Knit 2 together, knit 8, slip, slip, knit (2 decreases made).

Row 3: Knit 2 together, knit 6, slip, slip, knit (2 decreases made).

Row 4: Knit 2 together, knit 4, slip, slip, knit (2 decreases made).

Row 5: Knit 2 together, knit 2, slip, slip, knit (2 decreases made).

3 Draw yarn through the 4 remaining stitches. To avoid a bump at the top of your hat, consider tightening the tension on those last 4 stitches before pulling the yarn tail through them. Cut the wool roving/yarn, leaving a 61cm (24in) tail, and pull it all the way through, securing the top by pulling the tail firmly through the remaining 4 stitches.

4 Use your fingers to thread the wool roving/yarn tail through the edge stitches on either side, creating a back seam.

You can adjust this hat's shape after you've knitted it. Wool roving is easy to work with, but treat it gently.

Making up

Weave in both ends of the wool roving/yarn. If you're using wool roving, you may also choose to secure your ends after weaving them in by needle felting them into the underside of a stitch. This will create an invisible and permanent connection.

*See the **Needle felting wool roving** section for more specific instructions.*

Wool roving can remain durable if you keep your stitches tight and secure any loose ends.

tip

To create a more relaxed fit, try using multiple strands of yarn rather than wool roving.

tip

Because ribbon yarn can be slippery, make sure you don't drop any loops off your arm as you knit.

Essential information

Difficulty level
Moderate

Time to make
20 minutes

Finished size
86.5 x 6cm (34 x 2½in)

Materials
63m (69 yds) of chunky ribbon yarn, with 6 strands held together

43cm (17in) of curb chain in your preferred colour

Lobster clasp

Four 10mm jump rings

Tools
2 pairs of flat-nose jewellery pliers

Wire cutters

Scissors

Tension
2 stitches and 2 rows equals 10cm (4in).

This project was made with 1 ball of Lion Brand Yarns Martha Stewart Crafts Glitter Ribbon in Verdalite, 63m (69 yds).

Knitted necklace

Try the rope-like I-cord stitch with this quick and easy necklace. You don't need any jewellery-making experience, assembly requires just basic techniques.

How to make

Necklace

1 Divide the yarn into 6 equal lengths, and then rewind it into balls.

2 Cast on 3 stitches.

3 Transfer the stitches to your opposite arm by slipping them one at a time. When you finish, the working yarn should be on the same side as your elbow rather than on the same side as your hand.

4 Arm knit these 3 stitches, pulling the working yarn across the back of the piece before you knit the first stitch. This helps create the rope-like I-cord look.

5 Transfer the stitches back to your other arm. Note that you're only knitting the stitches off one arm, always beginning with the working yarn on the same side as your elbow.

6 Repeat the knitting and transferring steps, working an I-cord until the piece measures 40.5cm (16in), or your desired length, and then cast off.

7 Weave in all the ends.

Use a synthetic but bright ribbon yarn for this necklace, allowing the colour to stand out, no matter what you wear with it.

Don't panic if you weave in your ends but they **poke out** a bit. You can use a needle and thread to secure them in the centre of the I-cord.

Continued ➡

Jewellery findings

1 Grasp one side of a jump ring with your jewellery pliers and then grasp the other side with the second pair of pliers. Turn one wrist away from you, opening the jump ring, as shown in Figure 1. Don't open the jump ring by pulling the ends apart from each other, as this can weaken and deform the ring.

2 Repeat the previous step to open the other 3 jump rings.

3 Using the wire cutters, cut the chain into 2 equal lengths.

Making up

1 Attach the chain to the I-cord by slipping 1 jump ring into each end of the I-cord, working the jump ring through as many strands of ribbon yarn as possible.

2 Slip one end of a piece of chain onto this jump ring. Grasp one side of the jump ring with your pliers and then grasp the opposite side of the jump ring with the second pliers. Turn one wrist towards you, allowing the jump ring ends to meet, and close the jump ring.

3 Attach the clasp to the chain by catching the loose end of the chain and one half of the lobster clasp in another jump ring. Close this jump ring.

4 Repeat the previous three steps to attach the chain and the clasp to the other end of the I-cord.

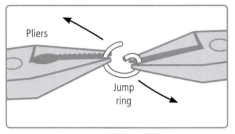

Figure 1 Open the ring by twisting the ends away from each other, not by pulling them apart.

You can use a different length of chain. Make sure it feels comfortable around your neck before you attach it to the necklace.

Essential information

Difficulty level
Moderate

Time to make
45 minutes

Finished size
Adult: Circumference equals 51cm (20in)

Child: Circumference equals 40.5cm (16in)

Materials
30m (33 yds) of giant netted acrylic-blend yarn for each hat

Tools
Scissors

Tension
2 stitches and 3.75 rows equals 10cm (4in).

Each project was made with 2 skeins of Premier Yarns Couture Jazz in Denim, 15m (16.5 yds).

These hats are easy to assemble and fun to wear.

Ski hat

Who doesn't love a hat topped with a sprightly pompom? Plaited ties also add to this hat's charm. The pattern comes in two sizes: adult and child.

How to make

Adult size

1 Cast on 5 stitches.

2 Arm knit 15 rows.

3 Cast off all the stitches, leaving a 25.5cm (10in) yarn tail.

Child size

1 Cast on 4 stitches.

2 Arm knit 13 rows.

3 Cast off all the stitches, leaving a 25.5cm (10in) yarn tail.

Making up

1 Fold the fabric in half, right side out. Place the fold at the top and the cast-on and cast-off edges at the bottom. Use mattress stitch to seam one side – the hat's back when it's unfolded.

2 Weave in and trim all the ends.

Ties (make 2)

Cut three 46cm (18in) strands of yarn. Knot them to the hat's front corners. Plait the strands and then tie a knot.

Pompom

Make a 5cm (2in) pompom and tie it to the crown of the hat with a thinner piece of yarn. Figure 1 shows how to seam the hat, attach the ties, and add the pompom.

*See the **Making a pompom** section for more specific instructions.*

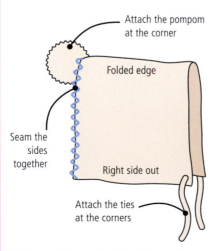

Attach the pompom at the corner

Folded edge

Seam the sides together

Right side out

Attach the ties at the corners

Figure 1 Seam the sides before adding the ties and the pompom.

tip

Make the pompom in a contrasting colour for a completely different look.

Making a pompom

If your project needs a little something extra, consider adding a pompom. You can make one in less than 15 minutes. The more you wrap in step 4, the better your finished pompom will look. To attach it to your project, pass a needle threaded with yarn through the central tie holding the pompom together.

What you'll need

• Small piece of cardboard
• Scissors
• Yarn

Pompom diameter

1 Decide how wide you'd like your pompom. Cut a piece of cardboard 15cm (6in) wide by the desired diameter of the pompom. Cut an opening from one short edge to the centre, reaching about three quarters of the way down the length.

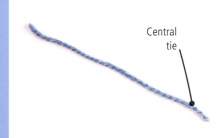

Central tie

2 Cut a 25cm (10in) length of yarn and set it aside. You'll use this as a central tie in step 5.

Knot the tie securely

5 Insert the central tie from step 2 through the space in the cardboard, and then tie it tightly around the wrapped yarn.

Size Considerations

For a pompom 5cm (2in) in diameter, cut the cardboard 15cm (6in) wide and 5cm (2in) tall. The taller the cardboard, the larger the pompom will be. If you want to make a smaller pompom, you can substitute a fork for the cardboard.

Leave space between the cardboard and the yarn

Keep the tension consistent

4 Wrap the yarn evenly around the cardboard, keeping the same amount of tension as you wrap. The more times you wrap the yarn round, the more dense the pompom will be.

Hold the yarn tail with your thumb

3 Place the yarn tail on the cardboard, lining up the end with the edge of the rectangle.

Use fabric scissors

6 Use your scissors to cut the loops on one side of the wrapping. Cut as evenly as possible to ensure all the strands are the same length.

Trim it

7 Repeat step 6 on the opposite side. Fluff the pompom, and then trim around it to make the edges even.

Open-weave bag

Knitting in garter stitch is easy, but suede lacing is challenging to work with and will expand your skill set. Buy it in bulk to avoid having to connect shorter lengths.

Essential information

Difficulty level
Moderate

Time to make
90 minutes

Finished size
Bag: 44.5 x 29cm
(17½ x 11½in)
Handle: 74cm (29in)

Materials
91m (100 yds) of 3mm faux suede lacing cord

46cm (18in) of 1.1m (45in)-wide non-stretch fabric for lining

Sewing thread

Tools
Sewing machine

Sewing needle

Pinking shears

Scissors

Pen or pencil

Ruler

Vanishing or wipe-off fabric marker

Cardboard: 44.5 x 29cm (17½ x 11½in)

Iron

Craft knife

Tension
3 stitches and 2 rows equals 10cm (4in).

This project was made with faux suede lacing cord in green, 92m (100 yds), 3mm wide.

How to make

Bag

1 Cast on 9 stitches, leaving a 76cm (30in) tail for seaming.

2 Beginning with a knit row, arm knit in garter stitch until the bag measures 89cm (35in) long, ending with a purl row. Cast off on a knit row, leaving another 76cm (30in) tail for seaming.

3 Fold the knitting in half lengthwise, so the cast-on and cast-off edges meet. You should have a long tail on each top edge. Seam each side by using the long tails left from casting on and casting off.

Handle

1 Cut 3 strands of suede faux lacing cord, each 2.75m (3 yds) long.

2 Hold the 3 strands with their ends lined up and then fold them in half, creating a loop. Slip the loop through one of the top edges of the bag where you seamed one of the sides. Slide the tails of the strands through the loop, securing one side of the handle to the bag.

Use a clothes peg to hold the unfastened end in place before firmly knotting it. This allows you to make the handle any length you prefer.

3 Plait the tails until the handle measures approximately 74cm (29in) long. You should then have a length of fringe remaining.

4 Being careful not to twist the plait, knot it to the opposite side seam.

5 Trim the handle fringe evenly.

Continued ➡

Make the lining

1 Place the bag on top of the piece of cardboard. Hold the top and bottom edges, pulling the bag to stretch it. Using a pen or pencil, trace around the outside of the bag. Using a ruler, draw straight lines for a seam allowance along the lines you sketched, creating a uniform lining template for cutting.

Cut out the template, then insert it into the bag, making sure it fits. If it doesn't, redraw the template, subtracting or adding the width or length as necessary.

2 Fold the fabric in half, with the right sides facing, and keeping the selvedges together. Place the template on top of the fabric, lining up the bottom edge of the template with the fold of the fabric.

Using a fabric marker, add a 3cm (1in) seam allowance along one side of the fabric and the top. Trace against the edge of the other side of the template.

Cut out the fabric using the guidelines.

3 Sew the side seams of the lining using a 1.5cm (¹/₂in) seam allowance, as shown in Figure 1. Finish the seams with pinking shears to prevent unravelling.

4 Fold the top of the lining over by 1.5cm (¹/₂in). Press with an iron, then fold over 1.5cm (¹/₂in) again. Press again with an iron.

5 Stitch around the top edge of the lining slightly less than 1.5cm (¹/₂in) from the edge.

Attach the lining

1 Turn the lining right side out, inserting it inside the bag and pinning it in place.

2 Use a sewing machine to sew around the top of the lining, catching as much of the suede as possible under the needle while securing the lining to the bag.

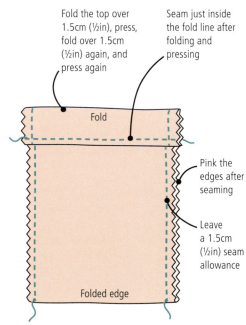

Fold the top over 1.5cm (½in), press, fold over 1.5cm (½in) again, and press again

Seam just inside the fold line after folding and pressing

Fold

Folded edge

Pink the edges after seaming

Leave a 1.5cm (½in) seam allowance

Figure 1 This is how the lining should look before you turn it right side out and put it inside the bag.

If you want to make the bag **sturdier,** you can use a more **durable material,** such as **rope,** or even hold **multiple strands of yarn** together.

tip
This bag isn't designed to hold heavy items. Check the label for how much weight the suede can support.

Essential information

Difficulty level
Moderate

Time to make
2 hours

Finished size
91cm to 1.2m (36 to 40in) chest

Materials
128m (140 yds) or 3.6kg (8lb) of hand-dyed merino wool roving for arm knitting

110m (120 yds) of chunky or giant 100% merino wool yarn for sewing up

Tools
Felting needle
Scissors

Tension
1.5 stitches and 2 rows equals 10cm (4in).

*This project was made with:
4 balls of Urban GypZ hand-dyed roving in Wild Raspberry, 32m (35 yds).*

1 skein of UrbanGypZ Bulky 3-ply yarn in Wild Raspberry, 110m (120 yds).

Chunky sweater

Wool roving creates mega stitches for this cosy top. It can take weeks to knit a sweater with needles. That's not the case with this design – guaranteed!

How to make

Front and back (work both the same)

1 Cast on 8 stitches.

2 Arm knit 9 rows.

3 Cast off all the stitches.

Sleeves (make 2)

1 Cast on 7 stitches.

2 Arm knit 6 rows.

3 Cast off all the stitches.

Although wool roving is delicate, you'll be struck by how sturdy this sweater looks and feels.

This jumper might look challenging, but it's quite easy: You knit four rectangular pieces and then assemble them using mattress stitch.

Continued ➡

tip

Because wool roving can develop entangled fibres called *neps*, keep your sweater looking tidy by shaving them off with a clothes shaver.

Making up

1 With the right sides of the back and front pieces facing upwards, as shown in Figure 1, use mattress stitch and the chunky yarn to seam 10cm (4in) in from each shoulder corner, leaving a 30cm (12in)-wide opening for the neck.

2 Find the centre stitch at the top of each sleeve, and use yarn to tie each sleeve to the shoulder seam through the centre stitch, as shown in Figure 2.

3 Stitch each sleeve to the body by using mattress stitch. Fold the piece as shown in Figure 3, and then use mattress stitch to sew the sleeve and side seams.

4 Weave in all the ends.

*See the **Needle felting wool roving** section for more specific instructions.*

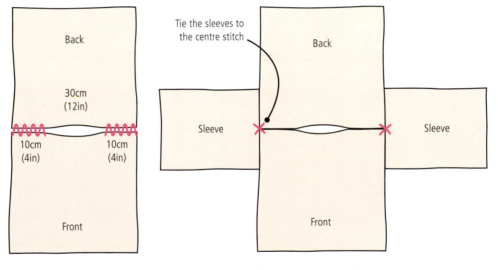

Figure 1 Use mattress stitch to seam the shoulders, leaving an opening for your neck.

Figure 2 Make sure all the pieces are right side up before tying a sleeve to each shoulder seam.

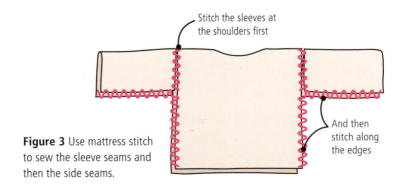

Figure 3 Use mattress stitch to sew the sleeve seams and then the side seams.

Home sweet home

From a bed for your four-legged friends and blankets to wrap yourself in on cold days to covers for cushions and lampshades, these projects will be focal points for any room.

Essential information

Difficulty level
Easy

Time to make
1 hour

Finished size
51 x 76cm (20 x 30in)

Materials
322m (352 yds) of super chunky yarn, with 6 strands held together (or 2 strands held together if using the chain plying technique)

Tools
Scissors

Tension
2 stitches and 3.75 rows equals 10cm (4in).

This project was made with 4 cones of Premier Craft-Tee Yarn in Blue Shades, 81m (88 yds).

Doormat

Super stretchy T-shirt yarn yields a hardy doormat that feels extra plush. Create your own T-shirt yarn to almost completely make this doormat with your own hands.

How to make

Doormat

1 Cast on 13 stitches.

First row: *Knit 1, slip 1 stitch with the yarn held in front. Repeat from * to the last stitch, knit 1.

Second row: Knit 1, *knit 1, slip 1 stitch with the yarn held in front. Repeat from * to the last 2 stitches, knit 2.

2 Repeat the first and second rows until your piece measures approximately 46cm (18in), or your desired length.

3 Cast off all the stitches.

4 Weave in and trim all the ends.

*See the **Making T-shirt yarn** and **Chain plying technique** sections for more specific instructions.*

Linen stitch gives this doormat a woven look, and you can even change colours every other row to create a different visual effect.

Reserve this doormat for indoor use. Because it's so thick, it won't dry quickly if it becomes wet outside.

tip

Knitting with 6 strands of T-shirt yarn held together will result in a doormat that can withstand heavy use.

Making T-shirt yarn

Making your own T-shirt yarn is fun. Different variables, such as how much stretch the fabric has and how wide you cut the strips, will determine how much fabric you need to start with to get the amount of yarn required for your project. The wider you cut the strips, the heavier the yarn weight.

What you'll need

- Several metres (yards) of jersey fabric
- Ruler
- Rotary cutter
- Self-healing cutting mat
- Fabric scissors

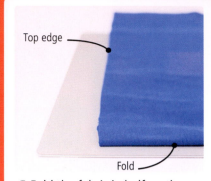

1 Fold the fabric in half on the self-healing cutting mat, with the selvedges meeting.

Top edge

Fold

Cut in from the fold

3 Roll the rotary cutter along the edge of the ruler and across the fabric, starting at the fold and stopping about 5cm (2in) from the selvedges. The cut should be parallel to the fabric's top edge.

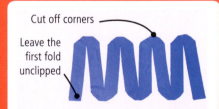

Cut off corners

Leave the first fold unclipped

6 At the folds and on the edges, use scissors to clip the corners of the cuts into 'curves', clipping across all but the first fold. These cuts don't have to look perfect because you won't see them once you stretch out the fabric later.

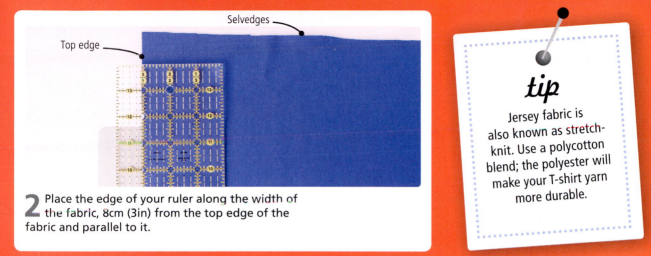

Top edge

Selvedges

2 Place the edge of your ruler along the width of the fabric, 8cm (3in) from the top edge of the fabric and parallel to it.

tip

Jersey fabric is also known as stretch-knit. Use a polycotton blend; the polyester will make your T-shirt yarn more durable.

4 Cut the fabric again, 8cm (3in) from the first cut and parallel to it, but this time starting at the selvedges and stopping 5cm (2in) from the fold.

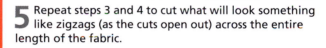

The cut width determines the yarn weight

5 Repeat steps 3 and 4 to cut what will look something like zigzags (as the cuts open out) across the entire length of the fabric.

7 You should now have one continuous strand of T-shirt yarn. Gently pull it to stretch it.

8 Roll the entire length of fabric into a ball and then use it as directed for any given T-shirt yarn pattern.

Using actual T-shirts

You can upcycle T-shirts into yarn, but the technique is different from the one described here because T-shirts are tubes of fabric, whereas fabric is a flat sheet. The advantage of using fabric to make yarn is that depending on how much fabric you start with, it yields far more yarn than an actual T-shirt.

Essential information

Difficulty level
Easy

Time to make
1 hour

Finished size
3.7m (4 yds) long

Materials
283m (310 yds) each of two different colours of chunky yarn, with 4 strands held together

Tools
Scissors

Tension
4 stitches and 2 rows equals 10cm (4in).

This project was made with: 2 balls of Bernat Softee Baby Chunky in Cream Puff, 142m (155 yds).

2 balls of Bernat Softee Baby Chunky in Buttercup, 142m (155 yds).

Pompom garland

Playful décor for a child's room or a festive accent for parties, this garland spells F-U-N. Make it as long as you like – striped or solid – and include cheerful pompoms.

How to make

Garland

Divide and rewind both yarn colours into 4 equal balls of each colour.

1 Cast on 5 stitches of one colour.

2 Arm knit all the stitches for 30.5cm (12in). Change colour and then knit for another 30.5cm (12in). Continue until the garland is your desired length, changing colours every 30.5cm (12in).

3 Cast off all the stitches.

4 Leave the yarn tails at both ends intact and use them for hanging the garland. Weave in the rest of the ends, or you can snip the ends to shorten.

Pompoms

Make 2 pompoms (in either one colour or two colours) and then tie a pompom to each end of the garland with separate strands of yarn.

*See the **Making pompoms** section for more specific instructions.*

Leaving yarn tails at the ends will give you ways to hang the garland.

For an even more jolly garland, weave a string of party lights into the strands to create a decoration that sparkles and glows!

tip

To help retain the rope-like shape of the knitted garland, give it a firm tug as you work and before you hang it.

tip

You can make the cushion cover with yarn, but you may find that wool roving provides a more sturdy and elegant look.

When seaming the edges together, pull them tight to close the seam, but don't pull so tightly that the edges pucker.

Essential information

Difficulty level
Easy

Time to make
1 hour

Finished size
40 x 40cm (16 x 16in)

Materials
Colour A: 82m (90 yds) of wool roving (or use super chunky yarn, with 4 strands held together)

Colour B: 82m (90 yds) of wool roving (or use super chunky yarn, with 4 strands held together)

40cm (16in) cushion pad

Tools
Scissors
Felting needle

Tension
2 stitches and 2 rows equals 10cm (4in).

This project was made with: 1 ball of Cloudborn Fibers Highland Roving in Stormy Skies, 82m (90 yds).

1 ball of Cloudborn Fibers Highland Roving in Dolphin Blue, 82m (90 yds).

Two tone cushion cover

This cushion cover offers practise with seaming. Using wool roving means a soft texture. Make a pair, choosing yarn colours or wool roving that coordinate with your décor.

How to make

Divide each wool roving/yarn colour into 4 balls.

First piece

1 Cast on 8 stitches with colour A.

2 Arm knit 7 rows.

3 Cast off, leaving a 51cm (20in) yarn tail for seaming.

Second piece

1 Cast on 8 stitches with colour B.

2 Arm knit 7 rows.

3 Cast off, leaving a 51cm (20in) yarn tail for seaming.

Making up

1 Place the two pieces side by side, with the right sides facing upwards.

2 Using one of the long tails you left earlier, seam one side of the pieces together with mattress stitch.

3 Turn the two pieces wrong sides together, and then sew the top and bottom edges together.

4 Weave in all the loose ends, except for the remaining seaming tail.

5 Turn the piece right side out, and then slip the cushion pad inside.

6 Seam the final edge of the two pieces together using the remaining yarn tail and mattress stitch. You might have to pull on the edges a little to get them to come together.

7 Weave in or needle felt any remaining wool roving/yarn.

See the Needle felting wool roving section for more specific instructions.

You can **customize** this pattern to fit any **rectangular** or **square** cushion.

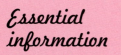

Essential information

Difficulty level
Easy

Time to make
30 minutes

Finished size
33 x 63cm (13 x 25in)

Materials
31m (34 yds) of 5mm
nylon rope

Tools
Scissors

Tension
2 stitches and 3.75 rows
equals 10cm (4in).

*This project was made with
nylon rope in white, 30m
(34 yds), 5mm in diameter.*

Mini hammock

Looking for a way to showcase a cuddly animal collection?
This hammock can fit in corners or along walls, offering ways
to keep toys off the floor, but still within reach.

How to make

Hammock

1 Cast on 10 stitches, leaving
a 38cm (15in) yarn tail.

2 Arm knit until the piece measures
approximately 63cm (25in).

3 Cast off all the stitches, and trim the
ends to approximately 38cm (15in).

Hanging mechanism

Loop the end through the opposite
side of the hammock from where the
rope is currently attached, so the rope
is doubled. Tie the end of the rope to the
point where the yarn is coming from. This
section of doubled rope creates 'handles'
you can attach to the walls, or the ceiling
for hanging the hammock.

This hammock is best used for lightweight
toys, despite being made with nylon rope, and it's
definitely not sturdy enough to hold people.

If you'd like a **less open look**
to your hammock, use a **thicker** rope.
This will also make the hammock **stronger**
and able to hold larger toys or items.

tip

You can make this hammock larger by casting on more stitches and then arm knitting additional rows.

tip

Use a bolster cushion pad that's slightly smaller than the cover's finished size to help make the knitted cover look thicker.

Essential information

Difficulty level
Easy

Time to make
30 minutes

Finished size
38 x 18cm (15 x 7in)

Materials
33m (36 yds) each of at least five different yarns, with all strands held together

Bolster cushion pad:
37.5 x 15cm (14¾ x 6in)

Tools
Tapestry needle
Scissors

Tension
1.75 stitches and 1.5 rows equals 10cm (4in).

This project was made with:

2 balls of Big Twist Yarns Natural Blend in Aged Brass, 90m (98 yds).

1 ball of Lion Brand Yarns Wool-Ease Thick & Quick in Butterscotch, 97m (106 yds).

1 ball of Lion Brand Yarns Heartland in Yellowstone, 230m (251 yds).

1 ball of Lion Brand Yarns Heartland in Bryce Canyon, 230m (251 yds).

1 skein of Lion Brand Yarns Homespun in Golden, 169m (185 yds).

1 skein of Buttercream Luxe Craft Rainbow Boucle in Mardi Gras, 568m (621 yds).

Bolster cushion cover

Combining complementary yarns adds visual texture to this quick knit project. You'll love how such a vibrant cushion cover can have a huge impact on any room design.

How to make

Pillow cover

1 Cast on 12 stitches.

2 Arm knit 12 rows.

3 Cast off all the stitches.

Making up

1 With 1 strand of sturdy but plain yarn, use mattress stitch to seam the two edges together, with the knit side of the piece on the inside and the purl side on the outside.

2 Thread a double length of the seaming yarn through all the cast-on stitches.

3 Close the cast-on end by using a double length of the seaming yarn, and threading that yarn through all the cast-on stitches.

4 Insert the bolster cushion pad into the knitted piece via the cast-off end.

When you hold the different yarns together before arm knitting, they should feel as thick, or thicker, than a super chunky yarn.

5 Cinch the cast-on edge opening closed by pulling the yarn and securing it to hold the stitches tightly.

6 Repeat this process for closing the cast-off end.

7 Weave in all the ends.

Using **thinner yarns** or **fewer strands** will allow **more** of the bolster cushion pad to **show**.

tip

Find an ideal place to comfortably hold this huge blanket as you arm knit it.

Snuggly blanket

Snuggly blanket

This is no ordinary blanket! You have the option to make it really large – as a double blanket – but if that feels too big, make a smaller size – as a single or lap blanket.

How to make

Double blanket (shown)

1 Cast on 25 stitches.

2 Arm knit in stocking stitch for 26 rows until your desired length is reached, or until you run out of yarn, making sure you unravel your yarn for the last row first, to prevent having a partial row.

3 Cast off all the stitches.

4 Weave in all the ends. For extra security, try needle felting the ends.

*See the **Needle felting wool roving** section for more specific instructions.*

Even the back of this huge blanket showcases an attractive stitch pattern.

Single blanket

Finished size: 1.1 x 1.9m (40 x 76in)

Materials: 206m (225 yds) or 5kg (11lb) of wool roving (or giant yarn)

Knit count: 14 stitches x 25 rows

Lap blanket

Finished size: 91cm x 1.1m (36 x 45in)

Materials: 137m (150 yds) or 3.4kg (7.5lb) of wool roving (or giant yarn)

Knit count: 12 stitches x 14 rows

Essential information

Difficulty level
Easy

Time to make
2 hours

Finished size
Double blanket: 1.9 x 2.1m (76 x 80in)

Materials
Double blanket: 274m (300 yds) or 7kg (15lb) of raw, unspun merino wool roving with a 23-micron count (or use giant yarn in the same amount)

Tools
Scissors

Tension
1.33 stitches and 1.33 rows equals 10cm (4in) or 8cm (3in) per stitch.

This project was made with 1 ball of Intreccio Giant Merino roving in Sea Foam, 274m (300 yds).

Essential information

Difficulty level
Easy

Time to make
2 hours

Finished size
60 x 60 x 25.5cm
(24 x 24 x 10in)

Materials (makes 1)
87m (95 yds) of super chunky polyester/cotton blend T-shirt yarn or polyester blend T-shirt yarn for one cushion cover

Cushion pad: 60cm (24in) square

Tools
Tapestry needle
Scissors

Tension
1.5 stitches and 1.75 rows equals 10cm (4in).

This project was made with: Handmade T-shirt yarn in heather grey, 5m (5.5 yds).

Handmade T-shirt yarn in teal, 5m (5.5 yds).

Cushion cover with tassels

Arm knitting is all about scale. And T-shirt yarn produces enormous stitches, ideal for sturdy covers for giant cushions. Immense tassels emphasize the corners.

How to make

Front and back (make 2)

1 Cast on 15 stitches.

Rib stitch row: Slip the first stitch, *purl 1, knit 1; repeat from * across the row for a 1 x 1 rib stitch.

2 Repeat the rib stitch for 10 more rows.

3 Cast off all 15 stitches in the 1 x 1 rib stitch pattern.

Making up

1 Place the wrong sides of the back and front together, matching all the edges. Using mattress stitch, seam together three sides of the cover: one set of sides, then the cast-on edges, and finally the other set of sides.

2 Insert the cushion pad into the cover.

3 Using mattress stitch, sew the cushion cover closed at the cast-off edges.

4 Weave in all the ends.

Tassels help the cushion cover and its corners look more polished.

Tassels

Make 4 tassels, each 15cm (6in) long. Tie or knot a tassel to each of the cushion corners with a separate piece of yarn.

*See the **Making tassels** section for more specific instructions.*

Making tassels

Tassels are simple adornments you can add to anything from home décor (such as cushions) to accessories (such as scarves). They look great at the corners of a project, but are equally sharp when attached along the length of a side. A tassel takes less than 15 minutes to make.

What you'll need

- A book as tall as the desired length of the finished tassel
- Scissors
- At least 2.7m (3 yds) of yarn

Knot

Loop

Short tail of the loop

Long tail of the loop

3 Cut a 61cm (24in) length of yarn, looping one end and holding it vertically against the tassel's tied end with your thumb.

tip

You can make your tassels in a colour that matches the project, or in a colour that will stand out.

Knot tightly

1 Wrap the yarn around the book 12 times. Cut a piece of yarn 15cm (6in) long, and tie it around the wrapped yarn.

Knotted end

Cut through the wraps

2 Cut through the wrapped yarn opposite the tied end.

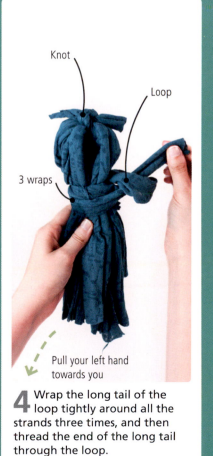

Knot

Loop

3 wraps

Pull your left hand towards you

4 Wrap the long tail of the loop tightly around all the strands three times, and then thread the end of the long tail through the loop.

Wrap

5 Pull the end of the short tail to tighten the loop. It should be tucked just beneath the wraps, locking the ends in place. (Tuck the end in if it's not completely camouflaged.)

Knot

Wrap

6 Trim the tassel ends so they're all the same length.

Essential information

Difficulty level
Easy

Time to make
45 minutes

Finished size
1.1m x 38cm (45 x 15in)

Materials
1.9m (210 yds) of super chunky yarn, with 3 strands held together

Pot or planter: 45cm (17½in) tall and 1.6m (62in) in circumference

Tools
Scissors
Plastic clips for assembly

Tension
4 stitches and 2 rows equals 10cm (4in).

This project was made with 3 balls of Red Heart Mixology in Ivory, 64m (70 yds).

Planter cover

Chunky moss stitch gives this highly textured piece a woven appearance. Not only will this cover liven up any plain pot, but it will also add a subtle focus to a room.

How to make

Cover

1 Cast on 10 stitches.

First row: Knit the first stitch. Purl the next stitch. Repeat this knit-purl sequence for the remainder of the row.

Second row: Create the moss stitch pattern by purling the knit stitches and knitting the purl stitches.

2 Repeat the first and second rows until the piece measures approximately 1.1m (45in).

3 Cast off all the stitches, leaving a 46cm (18in) yarn tail.

4 Seam the cast-on and cast-off edges together by using whip stitch.

Drawstrings

1 Cut two strands of matching yarn, each one measuring twice the pot's circumference.

2 Along one edge of the cover, beginning at the seam, weave one of the strands around the entire edge of the piece to create a drawstring for the top edge.

3 Along the other edge, beginning at the seam, weave the other strand around the entire edge of the piece to create a drawstring for the bottom edge.

Drawstring

Drawstrings allow you to adjust the cover size for planters with different circumferences.

Making up

1 Stretch the cover around the pot, using plastic clips as needed to help hold the cover in place.

2 Pull the top drawstring tightly, and then tie a knot to secure the cover in place. Pull and stretch the cover downwards and then pull the lower drawstring tightly to secure the bottom part. If the plant pot has a tapered base, the bottom can be pulled tighter than the top to fit. Knot tightly.

3 Weave in all the ends.

tip

You can match the yarn colour to your planter, or to the flowering plant's colour. Alternatively, be bold and use a contrasting shade.

tip

Flip the throw over to reveal a completely different texture on the reverse stocking stitch side.

Essential information

Difficulty level
Easy

Time to make
90 minutes

Finished size
1.5 x 1.7cm (60 x 65in)

Materials
872m (954 yds) of super chunky yarn, with 2 strands held together

Tools
Scissors

Tension
4 stitches and 2 rows equals 10cm (4in).

This project was made with 9 balls of Lion Brand Yarns Wool-Ease Thick & Quick in Glacier, 97m (106 yds).

Soft fringed throw

Loose stitches make this throw easy to create – perfect for a super quick gift. Each side has a different stitch texture, knit on one and reverse stocking stitch on the other.

How to make

Throw

1 Cast on 50 stitches.

2 Arm knit all the stitches until the throw measures 1.4m (55in).

3 Cast off all the stitches.

4 Weave in all the ends.

Fringe

Cut 2 strands of yarn, each approximately 25.5cm (10in) long, and then make a 12.5cm (5in) fringe evenly along the throw's top and bottom edges.

*See the **Making a fringe** section for more specific instructions.*

To make the fringe look neater, cut it a little longer than needed. After the fringe has been attached, trim across it in a straight line with a pair of sharp scissors.

Try knitting half the throw in one colour and the other half in another colour for an on-trend colour block look.

Lampshade cover

Clean lines in neutral tones make this cover bold and modern. Mount it wrong-side out on an oversized lampshade to showcase the reverse stocking stitch.

How to make

Cover

1 Cast on 9 stitches.

2 Arm knit all the stitches until the piece measures approximately 2.1m (80in). It will be a little smaller than the lampshade's circumference and height because the cover will be stretched open when it's attached. To change the cover's circumference, knit fewer or more rows according to the tension.

3 Cast off all the stitches, leaving a 46cm (18in) yarn tail.

4 Seam the cast-on and cast-off edges together by using whip stitch.

5 Weave in all the ends.

Drawstrings

1 Cut two pieces of matching yarn, making each one measure twice the shade's circumference.

2 Along one edge of the cover and beginning at the seam, weave one of the strands around the entire edge. This becomes the top edge.

3 Repeat this weaving process for the opposite edge. This becomes the cover's bottom edge.

4 Place the cover onto the shade, with the back of the piece facing outwards, stretching it so it completely covers the lampshade. (Displaying the reverse stocking stitch side gives the cover a grid-like texture.) Use clips as needed to hold the cover in place as it is fitted.

5 Pull the top drawstring tight, and then tie a firm knot to secure the cover in place. The drawstring should be concealed from sight inside the top of the shade, so you may need to shift the clips slightly to keep the cover from slipping as it's worked into place.

Pull and stretch the cover firmly downwards, and then pull the bottom drawstring tightly to secure the bottom part of the lampshade cover, making sure the drawstring is hidden from sight inside the bottom of the shade. Knot securely.

tip

Use large plastic clips to hold the cover in place while attaching it to the lampshade. This will help as you secure the drawstrings.

A drawstring ensures the cover remains securely in place.

tip

A ruler makes measuring your fringe easier. Changing the length of the fringe will give the rug a different vibe.

Essential information

Difficulty level
Easy

Time to make
1 hour

Finished size
81.5 x 91cm (32 x 36in)

Materials
Colour A: 271m (296 yds) of super chunky yarn, with 6 strands held together

Colour B: 271m (296 yds) of super chunky yarn, with 6 strands held together

Tools
Scissors

Tension
2 stitches and 3.75 rows equals 10cm (4in).

This project was made with: 4 skeins of Premier Mega Tweed in Gray, 68m (74 yds).

4 skeins of Premier Mega Tweed in Mint, 68m (74 yds).

Striped rug with a fringe

Making this project gives you a chance to practise adding a fringe, as well as changing colours after knitting several rows. Pick colours that complement your décor.

How to make

Rug

1 Cast on 17 stitches in colour A.

2 Arm knit 4 rows in colour A.

3 Switch to colour B and knit 4 rows.

4 Repeat steps 2 and 3 two more times.

5 Cast off all the stitches.

Fringe

Attach a fringe along the top and bottom of the rug. For each fringe, cut a 23cm (9in)-long strand of each colour. Hold both strands together while attaching the fringe. Trim the fringe evenly to 10cm (4in) long.

*See the **Making a fringe** section for more specific instructions.*

You can add a fringe that incorporates both colours used for the rug, just one colour from the project, or even another colour entirely.

Create your **own design** for this accent rug by **varying the length** of the stripes, or making it a longer runner.

Pet bed

After knitting a rectangle, you'll pick up and cast off stitches to make the bed's sides. Loop the tails through the corners and then tighten them to form a basket.

How to make

Base

1 Cast on 6 stitches.

2 Arm knit 6 rows.

3 Cast off all the stitches.

Sides

The edgings are worked one at a time along each edge of the bed base.

1 To make the first edging, pick up 4 centre stitches along the cast-off edge of the knitted base, missing the first and last stitches. Cast off these 4 stitches, leaving at least a 20.5cm (8in) yarn tail from the last cast-off stitch.

2 To make the next edging, pick up 4 centre stitches along the cast-on edge of the knitted base, missing the first and last stitches. Cast off these 4 stitches, leaving at least a 20.5cm (8in) yarn tail.

3 To make the side edgings, pick up 3 stitches, centred along one side of the base. Cast off these 3 stitches, leaving at least a 20.5cm (8in) yarn tail.

Don't worry about shaping this bed as your pet will stretch it to his or her liking.

4 Pick up 3 stitches along the other side edge of the base. Cast off these 3 stitches, leaving at least a 20.5cm (8in) yarn tail from the last cast-off stitch.

Continued ➔

tip

Merino wool is the most common type of wool roving commercially available and comes in many different colours.

Making up

Refer to Figure 1 as you work.
(It doesn't matter which way the
stocking stitch side faces.) Using the
20.5cm (8in) cast-off yarn tails, connect
the two sides of each corner together
by looping the tail through the first
stitch of the connecting side piece and
then tucking the tail back into the last
cast-off stitch on the tail side. This
creates a seamless edge to the cast off.

Weave in all the ends. Shape the bed
so the stocking stitch side is visible
inside the bed. If desired, needle felt
the ends of the wool roving for a more
secure connection.

See the **Needle felting wool roving**
section for more specific instructions.

Merino wool
roving is exceptionally
comfy and snuggly
—on discovering this bed,
your pet will claim it
immediately.

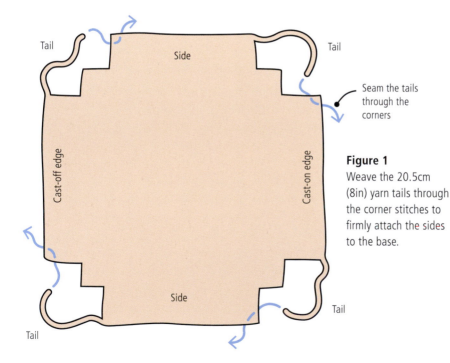

Tail

Side

Tail

Seam the tails
through the
corners

Cast-off edge

Cast-on edge

Figure 1
Weave the 20.5cm
(8in) yarn tails through
the corner stitches to
firmly attach the sides
to the base.

Tail

Side

Tail

Tail

tip

Try other less
expensive wool
roving for this
pet bed, such
as Corriedale,
Shetland, or
common
domestic roving.

tip

Because this beanbag has several different components, you don't need to make it in one sitting.

Beanbag

This beanbag has an unusual shape – the closed ends are perpendicular to each other, not parallel. Hypoallergenic polyester cord is ideal for this project.

How to make

Beanbag

1 Prepare 3 separate balls of cord, each 200m (219 yds) long. Cut 3m (3 yds) of cord from each ball. Set them aside to use to seam the beanbag sides together.

2 Cast on 18 stitches.

3 Arm knit until you run out of cord, ending with a full row. The piece should measure approximately 1.2m (48in) long.

4 Fold the cast-off edge to meet the cast-on edge, with the right side facing outwards. (The fold will be the bottom edge of the finished cover.) Use whip stitch to seam both sides of the beanbag while holding together all three

of the 3m (3-yd) cords set aside earlier. Make sure the ends of the cords are properly knotted to the piece so they don't come loose later.

5 Sew buttons to the right side of the open top edge. Fold the piece so the side seams are one above the other and run along the centre of the work instead of the edges. Evenly space the buttons before attaching them. Attach the first one along one seam line, with the others about 10cm (4in) away from it.

6 Weave in any loose ends. Carefully run the tips of each cord through the flame of the lighter to prevent them fraying.

Attach the buttons, evenly spaced, along the opening after arranging the side seams, so they're aligned in the centre of the work.

Continued

Inner casing

1 As shown in Figure 1, join the short ends of the pieces of fabric with the zip, centring the zip along the seam, and leaving the fabric at either end unsewn.

2 Open up the zip. Turn the pieces of fabric inside out. Pin the long sides and then stitch them, as shown in Figure 2. Finish the seams with pinking shears to prevent fraying.

3 Fold the fabric as shown in Figure 3, making sure the seams sewn in the previous step are no longer on the sides, but are in the centre. Stitch closed the

short open end. Finish the seams with pinking shears, and then turn the casing right side out.

4 Stuff the casing with your chosen filling and then zip the casing closed, as shown in Figure 4.

Finishing

Place the filled inner casing into the knitted beanbag, and then button the beanbag to close it. The buttons can be pushed through any corresponding stitch to secure.

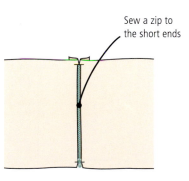

Sew a zip to the short ends

Figure 1 Use a ruler to ensure you centre the zip along the seam.

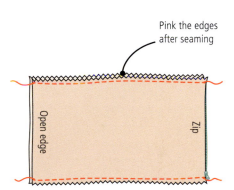

Pink the edges after seaming

Open edge

Zip

Figure 2 Make sure you open up the zip before seaming the side edges.

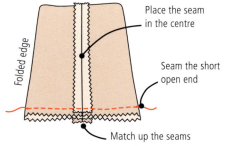

Folded edge

Place the seam in the centre

Seam the short open end

Match up the seams

Figure 3 Fold the fabric so the side seams meet in the centre.

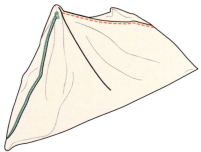

Figure 4 Turn the casing right side out, filling it with your chosen material before putting the casing inside the beanbag.

Concentric squares rug

This project has you knitting in all directions. After making a central square in one colour, you'll rotate the piece several times to add stitches in a different colour.

How to make

Colour A: Inner-centre square

1 Cast on 5 stitches in colour A.

2 Arm knit 6 rows.

3 Cast off all the stitches.

Colour B: Middle square

1 Pick up the stitches for Side 1 as follows: Turn the piece 90°. Using colour B, pick up and arm knit 6 stitches along the edge of the colour A square.

2 Arm knit 6 rows.

3 Cast off all the stitches.

4 Pick up the stitches for Side 2 as follows: Turn the piece 90°. Using colour B, pick up and arm knit 8 stitches along the colour B section just worked and along the edge of the colour A square.

5 Arm knit 6 rows.

6 Cast off all the stitches.

7 Pick up the stitches for Side 3 as follows: Turn the piece 90°. Using colour B, pick up and arm knit 8 stitches along the edge of the colour B section and the colour A square.

8 Arm knit 6 rows.

9 Cast off all the stitches.

10 Pick up the stitches for Side 4 as follows: Using colour B, pick up and arm knit 18 stitches along the colour B strip, the colour A square, and the colour B strip.

11 Arm knit 6 rows.

12 Cast off all the stitches.

The log cabin knitting technique builds on a central square, allowing you to add flourishes once you construct the central square.

Continued ➡

This project will give you ample opportunity to practise several arm knitting techniques, including changing colours.

Colour C: Outer square

1 Pick up the stitches for Side 1 as follows: Turn the piece 90°. Using colour C, pick up and arm knit 18 stitches along the edge of the colour B square.

2 Arm knit 6 rows.

3 Cast off all the stitches.

4 Pick up the stitches for Side 2 as follows: Turn the piece 90°. Using colour C, pick up and arm knit 6 stitches along the edge of the colour C section and 18 stitches along the edge of the colour B square.

5 Arm knit 6 rows.

6 Cast off all the stitches.

7 Pick up the stitches for Side 3 as follows: Turn the piece 90°. Using colour C, pick up and arm knit 6 stitches along the edge of the colour C section and 18 stitches along the edge of the colour B square.

8 Pick up the stitches for Side 4 as follows. Using colour C, pick up and arm knit 30 stitches along the colour C strip, the colour B square, and the colour C strip.

9 Arm knit 6 rows.

10 Cast off all the stitches.

11 Weave in and trim all the ends.

tip

You can always experiment with other yarns, and fewer or more colours, depending on your confidence and skill level.

tip

Position all the side panels in the same direction, so they'll stretch at the same rate and stay the same size once they're assembled.

Footstool cover

This cover can quickly add texture to everyday furniture. Its large stitches serve as the attachments, simply hook a corner stitch under the corresponding footstool leg.

How to make

Top panel

1 Cast on 8 stitches.

2 Starting with a knit stitch, alternate 1 knit stitch and 1 purl stitch, working all the stitches across the row.

3 Repeat step 2 seven times (for a total of 8 rows).

4 Cast off all the stitches.

Side panels

Repeat the steps for the top panel four more times to make 4 side panels.

Making up

1 Working on a flat surface, arrange the panels as shown in Figure 1, with the right sides facing upwards.

Make sure all the side panels face in the right direction (the cast-off edge is the top edge) to ensure the side seams remain the same size when stitched.

Attach the side panels to the top panel by using mattress stitch.

2 Position the cover on the stool. Stitch the side seams along the stool's corners by using mattress stitch.

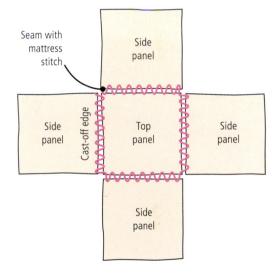

Figure 1 Arrange the panels with their right sides facing upwards, as shown here.

Add a **whimsical touch** by working each panel in a **different colour** – making this a **perfect accent** piece.

Essential information

Difficulty level
Moderate

Time to make
3 hours

Finished size
1.1 x 1.5m (42 x 60in)

Materials
151m (165 yds)
of jumbo netted
acrylic-blend yarn

Tools
Scissors

Tension
2 stitches and 3.75 rows
equals 10cm (4in).

*This project was made with
10 skeins of Premier Yarns
Couture Jazz in Olive,
15m (16.5 yds).*

Textured throw

You'll alternate knit rows with a few purl rows to create a reversible throw that looks almost horizontally ribbed. Netted yarn lends more loft and more warmth.

How to make

Throw

1 Cast on 24 stitches.

2 Arm knit 4 rows.

3 Purl 2 rows.

4 Repeat steps 2 and 3 five more times.

5 Arm knit 4 rows.

6 Cast off all the stitches.

7 Weave in and trim all the ends.

Alternating knit and purl stitches creates a throw that's not only beautiful and warm but also durable.

Probably the **hardest aspect** to this project is choosing which room, or piece of furniture you'll **accent with this throw.** Move it around your living space as needed – you'll find it can **fit anywhere.**

tip

Knit this throw in two different colours for a great colour block scheme.

tip

After knitting,
you could randomly
tie on little bells,
or add beads,
or prisms, which
reflect light.

Essential information

. . . .

Difficulty level
Moderate

Time to make
2½ hours

Finished size
91cm x 2.1m (36 x 84)

Materials
137m (150 yds) of
100% cotton DK yarn

Sewing thread to match the
chosen yarn colour

Solid-coloured sheer
curtain to match the
yarn colour: 1.3 x 2.1m
(50 x 84in)

Tools
Sewing needle

Sewing pins

Scissors

Tension
2 stitches and 2 rows
equals 10cm (4in).

*This project was made with
1 skein of Blue Sky Alpacas
Worsted Cotton in Bone,
137m (150 yds).*

Lacy curtain

Inspired by 1970s macramé, this airy curtain has a delicate pattern. Putting a solid-coloured sheer curtain behind the knitting allows its lacy effect to stand out visually.

How to make

. . . .

Curtain

1 Cast on 23 stitches loosely.

2 Arm knit 4 rows.

3 Purl 1 row.

4 *Knit 2 stitches together, yarnover; repeat from * to the last stitch and then knit the last stitch.

(To perform a yarnover, place the working yarn behind the arm holding the stitches and then immediately bring the yarn up, over, and around to the front.

This wraps it partially around your wrist from back to front.

You can then simply continue working as described in these instructions.)

5 Arm knit 1 row.

6 Purl 1 row.

7 Repeat the previous 8 rows three more times for a total of 24 rows.

8 Cast off all the stitches.

The yarnover technique creates an extra loop on your arm and results in a deliberate hole in the knitting. That creates the larger stitches.

Making up

Spread the cast-on end of the piece flat on your work surface. Put the sheer panel face down on the curtain, arranging it evenly and aligning the top and side edges of both curtains. Pin them together, and working with each cast-on stitch, use the needle and sewing thread to tack the cast-on end to the curtain.

Contributors

Stacey Budge-Kamison

Stacey Budge-Kamison is a fibre artist with a hand-crafted yarn business (UrbanGypZ.com) that specializes in edgy yarns and fibres for knitters, crocheters, weavers, and handspinners, with a focus on sustainable fibres and unexpected colourways. Stacey's studio is located in Raleigh, North Carolina, USA, where she lives with her husband, two cats, and two dogs.

Mari Chiba

Mari Chiba started knitting while serving in Armenia as a Peace Corps volunteer. During the long, cold winters, she'd knit herself a blanket to keep warm. This led her to start designing knitting patterns. Mari has had designs published in *Twist Collective*, *Knitscene*, *Interweave Knits*, *Knitty*, and many other publications. You can follow her adventures in knitting and designing on her blog at mariknits.com.

Jennifer Dickerson

Jennifer Dickerson is a freelance writer, knitting and crochet pattern designer, and all-round craft enthusiast. She authors the popular Fiber Flux blog (FiberFluxBlog.com), sharing patterns, articles, book and yarn reviews, and tutorials. Jennifer also teaches crochet and knitting techniques on her growing YouTube channel. Jennifer is the author of *Mini Flower Loom Crafts: 18 Super Simple Projects* and contributed designs to *American Gift Knitting* and *Knitting 2014 Day-to-Day Calendar*. She designs regularly for *I Like Crochet* magazine, and she was named a top blogger by Prime Publishing in 2012, 2013, 2014, and 2015.

Haven Evans

Haven Evans lives in Pennsylvania, USA and is a busy mother of three who works from home full time. She recently discovered that arm knitting is a fun and easy way to de-stress at the end of the day, and she has since pursued this hobby with enthusiasm.

Ashley Little

Ashley Little is a craft writer and editor by day and a serial crafter by night. Her blog TheFeistyRedhead.com explores knitting, crocheting, sewing, and crafting, and it includes her own original patterns and reviews. Ashley's also a regular contributing writer for *Craftsy* (craftsy.com), and she authored *Chunky Knits*.

Rugilė Mickevičiūtė

Rugilė Mickevičiūtė hails from Lithuania and has always been driven by the desire to create attractive things. She has found that her true calling is to craft items that make people's homes cosy and comfortable. She likes objects that are exclusive, unique, and authentic, and she wants her own designs to reflect this attitude. Rugilė loves soft shapes and materials, large spaces, and low furniture, so it's no surprise she makes chunky Scandinavian-style poufs, beanbags, and cushion covers in various colours, as showcased on her website puffchic.com. She sells her creations on Etsy at etsy.com/shop/Puffchic.

Emilie Odeile and Ken Chapin

Emilie Odeile and Ken Chapin are the team behind a business called Intreccio. This Italian word means to weave together, interlace, or intertwine, and it perfectly describes the work Emilie and Ken are doing at their design studio located at the base of one of Colorado's highest peaks. Emilie loves to knit, and Ken's pretty happy in the wood shop. They've combined her many years of designing unique knitwear for private and celebrity clients with his artistic vision and masterful use of tools to create a full collection of giant knitting needles, a growing selection of patterns, and a vibrant community of giant knitters. You can see more of their work at etsy.com/shop/Intreccio.

Acknowledgments

The publisher is grateful to the following companies for contributing yarns for some of the projects in this book: Cloudborn Fibers, Lion Brand Yarns, Plymouth Yarn, and Red Heart.

Thanks to Ashley Little, the consultant who wrote the "Materials, tools, and techniques" section.

Special thanks to Grayson Davis, Philippa Nash, Gina Rodgers, Lexy Scheele, Anissa Zajac, and Everly Zajac for modelling the projects, as well as Lindsay Dobbs for modelling the techniques, and for Rocky – that little pooch who turned into a supermodel when the camera pointed at him.

DK UK
Project Editor Kate Meeker
Senior Art Editor Glenda Fisher
Angliciser and Editor Katharine Goddard
Jacket Designer Harriet Yeomans
Senior Producer, Preproduction Tony Phipps
Producer Olivia Jeffries
Creative Technical Support Sonia Charbonnier
Managing Editor Stephanie Farrow
Managing Art Editor Christine Keilty

DK US
Publisher Mike Sanders
Associate Publisher Billy Fields
Acquisitions Editor Nathalie Mornu
Development Editor Christopher Stolle
Technical Editor Rita Greenfeder
Book Designer Hannah Moore
Art Director for Photography Becky Batchelor
Photographers Katherine Scheele (projects)
and Becky Batchelor (techniques)
Stylist Anissa Zajac
Illustrator Philippa Nash
Prepress Technician Brian Massey
Proofreader Monica Stone

First published in Great Britain in 2016 by
Dorling Kindersley Limited
80 Strand, London, WC2R 0RL

Copyright © 2016 Dorling Kindersley Limited
A Penguin Random House Company
10 9 8 7 6 5 4 3 2 1
001–298763–Nov/2016

A CIP catalogue record for this book
is available from the British Library.
ISBN: 978-0-2412-8348-6

Printed and bound in China.

All images © Dorling Kindersley Limited
For further information see: www.dkimages.com

A WORLD OF IDEAS:
SEE ALL THERE IS TO KNOW

www.dk.com